Milo Mahan

Palmoni

Or, the numerals of scripture, a proof of inspiration. A free inquiry.

Milo Mahan

Palmoni
Or, the numerals of scripture, a proof of inspiration. A free inquiry.

ISBN/EAN: 9783337183332

Printed in Europe, USA, Canada, Australia, Japan

Cover: Foto ©ninafisch / pixelio.de

More available books at **www.hansebooks.com**

Palmoni;

or, the

NUMERALS OF SCRIPTURE

A PROOF OF INSPIRATION.

A FREE INQUIRY.

By M. MAHAN, D.D.,

ST. MARK'S-IN-THE-BOWERY PROFESSOR OF ECCLESIASTICAL HISTORY IN THE GENERAL THEOLOGICAL SEMINARY.

He created Wisdom, and saw her, and *numbered* her, and poured her upon all His works. Why else is He styled PALMONI (Dan. viii, 13), which is rendered in the margin of our English Bibles, *The Numberer of Secrets, or the Wonderful Numberer?*—BIBLIOTHECA BIBLICA, iv, p. 8.

NEW YORK:
D. APPLETON AND COMPANY,
443 & 445 BROADWAY.
LONDON: 16 LITTLE BRITAIN.
1863.

ENTERED, according to Act of Congress, in the year 1863, by
D. APPLETON AND COMPANY,
In the Clerk's Office of the District Court of the United States for the Southern District of New York.

'Ο Θεὸς μάλιστα πάντων γεωμετρεῖ.

"He created Wisdom, and saw her, and *numbered* her, and poured her upon all His works."—Ecclus. i, 9.

"Thou hast ordered all things in measure, and *number*, and weight."—Wisdom xi, 30.

"Of His understanding there is no *number*."—Ps. cxlvii, 5.

"Est autem, et præter illam alia quam nos attulimus, nova per numeros philosophandi institutio, antiqua illa quidem, et à priscis Theologis, a Pythagora præsertim . . . . prioribusque Platonicis observata: sed quæ hac tempestate, ut præclara alia, posteriorum incuria sic exolevit, ut vix vestigia ipsius ulla reperiantur."—Johan. Picus de Mirandula, quoted in *Bibliothec. Biblic.* iv, p. 9.

PREFACE.

This is called "a *free* Inquiry," because it is strictly such: the subject with which it deals being entirely an open question, and the investigation of it being conducted with all due deference (I trust) to prejudices which it may disturb, but without any appeal to *mere* authority, whether of the early Church or the modern.

In some parts of the work the ground has been broken by others, and I have of course availed myself of the advantage of their labors. The chronology, for example, has been learnedly explored by Browne, in his *Ordo Sæclorum*, a book frequently referred to in the course of this Inquiry. But I have not simply followed Browne. A mistake of his, in one important point, led me to work out the whole scheme *de novo et ab ovo*. The result has been that, with the exception of this one point, I find my effort to harmonize in the main with his, and so far as the principle is concerned to be more than corroborative of his remarkable conclusions.

In that part of the work which will be the newest to most readers, and in which I may have to entreat them to "strike, but hear," the leading idea is one familiar to the early Church. It does not appear, however, that it was ever subjected to a rigorous scientific examination.

As to the connection between these parts, the application of mystic numbers as a key to sacred dates, I do not know whether any one has been before me. The famous Mirandula professed to have found the secret of Spiritual Arithmetic: but what he made of the subject, or whether he put his discoveries to the severe proof of connecting them with Chronology, I have not been able to ascertain.

Hoping the effort may be useful, at least in calling attention to an interesting subject, I submit it to the judgment of the candid and thoughtful reader.

M. MAHAN.

GENERAL THEOLOGICAL SEMINARY, N. Y.,
June 9th, 1863.

CONTENTS.

CHAPTER		PAGE
I.	General View of the Subject,	9
II.	The Six Judgments and Six Days of Preparation for Christ's Kingdom,	16
III.	The World before the Flood a Type of Judaism,	20
IV.	The Way to ascertain the Bible Chronology,	24
V.	Chronology of the Third and Fourth Days,	28
VI.	Chronology of the Fifth Day: the Judges,	31
VII.	Chronology of the Fifth Day: the Kings,	35
VIII.	The Sixth Day: Daniel's Seventy Weeks: Two Chronological Tables,	43
IX.	Symmetrical Periods of the World before the Flood and the Levitical Dispensation,	48
X.	Symmetries of the Abrahamic, Israel-Judah, Jerusalem, and other Periods,	53
XI.	Philosophic Principles involved in this Inquiry,	62
XII.	The Dominical Number Eight examined and tested,	71
XIII.	The Numbers Seven, Nine, Thirteen, tried by the same Criterions,	86
XIV.	The Meanings of a few other Numerals briefly indicated,	109
XV.	The Mystic Numbers a Key to the Sacred Chronology: The three Millenniums in One,	120

CHAPTER	PAGE
XVI. The Scheme Supernatural and Divine, . . .	135
XVII. Relations of Sacred and Profane Chronology: the Age of the World: The Bible a History of the Supernatural, .	148
Appendix A—Bishop Butler and Isaac Williams, . .	163
Appendix B—A Table of Minor Dates, . . .	167
Appendix C—The Number Six, ...	175

PALMONI;

OR,

THE NUMERALS OF SCRIPTURE.

CHAPTER I.

GENERAL VIEW OF THE SUBJECT.

As the subject of this Inquiry is one that will be new to most readers, and as the principal drift of it will not appear all at once, it seems proper to state beforehand, what are some of the results which may be expected from it. And this I will do in a hypothetical form.

Suppose it had been our fortune to alight on some valuable historical documents of the olden time; suppose these documents, being examined, were found to contain a very precise Chronology, covering a period of thousands of years, and interspersed with lively narratives of the most interesting character; suppose further, that the contents of these documents were of a kind to provoke much discussion, to excite curiosity, to satisfy in part, and in part to baffle, that eager desire of knowledge which is natural to man: we can readily imagine, in such a case, what pains would be taken to make out with precision the Record thus brought before us, to sum up its peculiarities, to ascertain, if possible, the principle on which it was constructed.

Now the Bible is such a collection of ancient documents. It contains a Chronology such as has been described. Yet, strange to say, the effort to draw out that Chronology as a whole, to present it honestly as it is, and to examine and account for its characteristic features, is even to this day almost a new thing. There have been plenty of attempts to *amend* the Chronology of the Bible. To set it forth symmetrically, in its own proper guise, has been aimed at by few, and has never perhaps been achieved with entire success by any.*

Suppose further, that, an honest effort being made to give this Chronology as it is, it should thereupon appear to abound in curious *parallelisms*, in strange *coincidences*, in *symmetries* of the most remarkable and rhythmical description. Suppose it should be marked in every part by the recurrence of certain mystical terms of years, not in a random way, but at intervals and in proportions elaborately exact. Suppose, in short, that this Chronology should prove to be constructed on a system. Suppose, finally, that a key to this system should appear in certain numerals, such as Five, Seven, Eight, Thirteen, and the like, which can be shown, by a rigorous induction and by scientific tests, to have a definite *spiritual* meaning, over and above their arithmetical value.

* Browne's *Ordo Sæclorum* is the nearest approach to a success; but in one or two points, as I expect to show, he has substituted conjecture for *facts*, preferring epochs of his own to those given him in Scripture.

In such a case, the proof of *Design* in the peculiarities of the Numerals of Scripture would be of such a character as no one could candidly disregard: the notion of chance coincidences would be absolutely excluded.

But suppose further, that the system thus discovered should be *latent*, in the same sense that the laws of nature are latent: in other words, that it should be obvious enough when once pointed out, but of a character to elude casual observation, and discoverable only on the application of certain experimental tests. Suppose *one* key to this system should be found in two or three *seemingly casual* utterances of the New Testament; and *another* key in two or three well-known dates of ordinary history. Suppose, generally, that its secret should lie, like the secret of Samson's strength, in those parts of Holy Scripture which critics are apt to consider a fair subject for their scissors, which being "unimportant," they can clip and pare at pleasure: in the *obiter dicta*, as such passages are learnedly called, or in texts "manifestly corrupt," or "totally irreconcilable," or branded with any other of those phrases by which interpreters put the blame of their own stupidity upon the "sure word" of God.

In such a case, there would be decided evidence of a *supernatural* Design in the Numerals of Scripture.

Suppose, finally, that the system should be found not only consistent with itself, but in harmony with the general scheme of nature and revelation; that it should be found to ramify into the *minutiæ* of Scripture names and Scripture types, and into the dates connected with those names and the numbers connected with those types, and should seem to run through the whole of the sacred Text from Genesis to Revelation, in fibres as minute but as organic as the capillaries of the human body; nay, should occasionally take hold of things outside of Scripture times, and, overleaping hundreds of years between, should seize upon ordinary history *precisely at those points,* where, *supposing the system to be divine, it might be expected* to seize on it.

The supposition may seem extravagant. And I do not profess to be able to make it good to the utmost. Supposing, however, that it can be proved even in part, and that in such instances as are capable of being *tested mathematically* it should be shown to hold true, then the evidence of a *supernatural element* in Scripture, of a supernatural life pervading its organism, would not at all fall short of a scientific demonstration.

The present Inquiry is an effort in that direction. It does not pretend, however, to cover the whole ground. It is an examination of *one little corner* of a vast field of inquiry: a field more familiar to the early Church than to Christians of our times—the great and fertile field of the Symbolism of Scripture.

The Inquiry divides into three parts, which, as originally undertaken, were three separate investigations, begun at different times and from different motives, with no idea when they were begun that they would be found to be connected.

The first is merely a summary of the Six Epochs, and Six Days of Preparation for Christ's Kingdom: an arrangement adopted by the writer many years ago, partly for its convenience, and partly for the beautiful analogy it presents to the Six Days of Creation.

The second is a simple summing up of the dates and periods given in the Hebrew Scriptures. This was undertaken with a view to correct two or three obvious errors in Browne's *Ordo Sæclorum*, and with an idea that, the mistakes of this ingenious author being corrected, the *symmetries* which he points out, would prove to be delusive. The result, however, was entirely the opposite. Few of the "parallelisms" were touched by the correction : while many, not noticed by Browne and *of a more systematic character* than those which he has noticed, were brought out to view. His mistakes, in fact, conceal the most beautiful of the parallels : and though he gives instances enough to show that there is something very remarkable in the sacred "times and seasons," yet there are hardly enough to prove the principle that seems to pervade the entire scheme.* In the table of dates, as corrected in the present work, the general plan comes out so clearly, that it may be taken in at a glance.

The third branch of the Inquiry is a curious, and, I fear, may be thought a rather frivolous one. It is an examination into a point familiar to the early Church, and not without interest to some of our "matter-of-fact" moderns.† It began with an attempt to ascertain how far the strange "coincidences" connected with the so-called *Dominical Number, Eight*, are capable of rigid proof, or are merely oddities of that kind which may amuse an idle moment, but from a more serious point of view are unworthy of regard. Having investigated *Eight*, I was led on to take up *Seven*, with the

---

* Of these mistakes, however, there is only one that affects the general results. The others balance one another, and are comparatively unimportant.

† See Wordsworth's "New Testament," *Notes* on 1 Peter iii, 21 ; 2 Pet. ii, 5 ; Luke xxiv, 1 ; Matt. x, 2 ; John xxi, 11.

same object in view. This brought me to the examination of some other "sacred" numbers. I have not given *all* the results of this inquiry. Those that I have given, however, are fair samples of the rest, and may serve to show, if nothing more, that the early Fathers had some excuse for their devotion to this curious branch of study.

It was after I had made some progress in the third of these inquiries, that I noticed how intimately they were connected: how admirably the Table of Dates fell in with the scheme of Days and Epochs, and what a light the "sacred Numbers" shed on the peculiarities of the Table of Dates.

With these remarks, I invite the reader to accompany me on a short excursion into this region of sacred Chronology. It is not as dry a field as most people imagine. There are flowers and fruits in it. And though the "flowers" may be partly of that kind which a learned and devout fancy can create at pleasure, yet many of them *may* be, and some of them doubtless are, of His handiwork who orders the "times and the seasons," Who numbers the very hairs upon our heads, Who determines man's days and the number of his months,* and Who may intentionally have clothed the otherwise dry details of Time's progress with something appealing to the imagination, out of that same abounding goodness which furnishes springs in the desert, or hangs the delicate and ethereal harebell upon the face of the bare rock.

And I may say in conclusion, that the difficulties of the inquiry are less than might be supposed. An English Bible and Concordance, a moderate facility in

* Job. xiv, 5.

the rule of simple addition, access to a few of the settled dates of ordinary history, and a willingness to trust one's own rather than other people's eyes, is all the critical apparatus that will be needed for our purpose. Perhaps, also, I might ask the reader to divest his mind of any undue and superstitious bias against the words "sacred," "typical," "mystical," or the like : * for if all nature is a mystery, if there are 'sermons in stones, and books in the running brooks,' surely we may expect to find, even in the *arithmetic* of Scripture, "more things than are dreamed of in our philosophy."

* The authority of a scholar, so learned, sober, and judicious, as Dr. Christopher Wordsworth, ought to have weight against mere *prejudices* on this subject. In his *Notes* on the New Testament, that noble contribution to Biblical scholarship, he touches *cautiously* on this branch of interpretation, but nevertheless feels constrained to bear witness to his sense of its value. His opinion is thus summed up : "The symbolical meaning of *Numbers* in Holy Scripture deserves more study and attention than it has received in recent times." Note to Matt. x, 2. See also the Appendix at the end of this volume.

CHAPTER II.

THE SIX JUDGMENTS AND SIX DAYS.

Among the many events in Sacred History which might be selected as convenient Epochs, there are six which stand out with a prominence peculiar to themselves: six, which are eminently typical of the last great Epoch, the coming of the Son of Man to judge the world.

They are all Epochs of Divine Judgment: of Judgment in its two aspects, "*salvific* to all who obey, and *destructive* to them who disobey."

I. There is *the expulsion from Eden*, with its mercy to man, its severity to the Tempter, and its waving fiery swords of Cherubim, the close of a Day *which has no chronological limits*, the period of the abode in Paradise. The Day thus closed, being the first and the eighth, the day of light prefiguring the day of the Resurrection, was in a peculiar sense "made" by God Himself. In it, He walked in the midst of the garden. We may distinguish it therefore as *The Lord's Day*. In chronology, we are obliged to reckon it, as we reckon eternity, simply by a blank or zero.

The Judgment which closes it serves at the same time to introduce the second, or *Adam's Day*.

II. There is *the Flood*, in which the wicked are condemned, and the righteous are saved, " by water." This is the decline of Adam's and the rise of *Noah's Day:* the transition point of the second and third great periods.

III. There is the fiery *overthrow of Sodom and Gomorrah*, in which mercy still strives with judgment, " a few " being saved, yet " so as by fire." This is the vanishing point of Noah's, and the dawn of *Abraham's Day:* Abram receiving at that crisis the name Abraham, with the covenant of circumcision.

IV. There is *the Judgment upon Pharaoh*, the Baptism unto Moses in the cloud and in the sea. This is the end of the Abrahamic period, and the beginning of the *Day of Moses*.

V. There is *the Destruction of Jerusalem and Solomon's Temple*, with the captivity in Babylon, and the purgation of the chosen people from the sin of idolatry. This is the end of the Mosaic era, and the sunrise, as it were, of *the Day of the Prophets*.

VI. There is *the final desolation of the Temple*, with the abolition of Levitical worship, and the deliverance of the Church from Judaism. This is " the evening " of the Prophetic term, and " the morning " of *the Day of the Son of Man*.

Each of these Epochs, marked by a judgment of mercy and of wrath, stands midway between an " evening " and a " morning," between the waning of an old, and the waxing of a new dispensation. In the expressive style of the Hebrew, " It was evening and it was morning, day one—day two "—or whatever it might be.

The Epochs, then, are mere points in sacred history.

And as there is no abruptness in the order of nature or of grace, the periods between which they stand melt into one another by a gradual change. Abram, for example, dwelt a time in Haran, and waited a time in Canaan, before he was called by the name Abraham. So, again, the Prophetic Day had a long "evening" before, and a long "morning" after, the Captivity in Babylon. It culminated, however, in Isaiah, Jeremiah, Ezekiel, and Daniel, the prophets of that crisis; and the time of its consolatory power was in the long interval of waiting that preceded the coming of the Messiah.

The epochs, in short, are but the crests of the great waves of human history. The waves themselves have their rise, their swell, and their decline; and it may be added, that as mariners tell us to look out for the *seventh* wave, because it comes with the accumulated force of the preceding six, so we are taught to look with trembling for the seventh grand epoch. It is to be the culmination and manifestation, the ridge and the crest, the outgrowth and upshot, of all the good and evil, the happiness and misery, of the ages which have gone before.

Now, in making out from Scripture the chronology of these six periods, we notice *first*, that the determining epochs are dated with emphasis and precision by the sacred writers; *secondly*, that the six fall naturally into three pairs or couples, the first pair standing in a close typical relation to the third.*

This "first pair" embraces the duration of the world

---

* I have not dwelt upon the analogy between these periods and the corresponding Days of Creation. Bishop Odenheimer points it out in his scholarly and ingenious "Primary Charge." It might be carried out into detail with the utmost minuteness. I

before the flood; the "third pair," the duration of the Levitical Economy.

As the inquiry which we are engaged in has everywhere a bearing upon the subject of *type relations*, it will be desirable, in this one case at least, to point out in a practical way what the word "typical" means, and how far we are warranted in applying it to certain periods.

will merely notice, however, that the first day is the creation of *light*, and the *separation between light and darkness :* in history, there is a like separation between *good and evil* in Eden, by the forbidden tree. The second day is that of the *firmament separating the waters above from the waters below*. Now, the waters in Holy Scripture are symbolical of the peoples. Historically, therefore, the second day drew the line between "the sons of God," the "waters above the firmament" of His covenant, and the "children of men," the "waters below." This second day, moreover, being the grand era of apostasy, it is perhaps *not accidental*, that in the Mosaic account of creation no blessing is pronounced upon the second day. It alone is not declared "good." The third day, the "dry land" appears, with *life* in its lower types. Historically, this day is the seed-time of the nations. See Gen. x. The fourth day, there are the "lights," or luminaries: in the sacred family, "the sun and moon and eleven stars" come forth as the signs of higher national life; in the world at large, there are similar signs of national organization. Order prevails. The candles are lighted, and *set upon candlesticks*. The fifth day is marked by an exuberance of higher life. The "waters bring forth abundantly." The "four great beasts," which afterwards "come up out of the sea," begin to live and breathe. Among the sacred people, there is the Law, the Theocracy, the Temple. On the sixth day, the "great beasts" come up on the land. The heathen empires are brought into contact with the true religion. Hence, a higher life, a higher and holier culture. The seeding and the spawning must now give place to the sacred nurture of the breast. —Such, in the main, are the six days of preparation.

CHAPTER III.

THE OLD WORLD THE TYPE OF JUDAISM.

In the chronology of the world before the flood, there is happily no difficulty. By simply adding up the terms which are given in Gen. v, 3–28, and vii, 2, we ascertain the sum of its duration to have been precisely 1,656 years.

But this world before the flood, with the water that overwhelmed it, stands in a typical relation to the " last times " of the preparation for Christ, the Levitical Dispensation.* " As the days of Noe were, " says our Lord, " so shall also the coming of the Son of Man be." So also St. Peter, in that remarkable passage in which he speaks of " the *long-suffering* of God in the days of Noah, while *the ark was a-preparing,* wherein few, that is, *eight* souls, were *saved by Water, the anti-type to which is now saving us,* even Baptism . . . . . by the Resurrection of Jesus Christ." Upon which passage Lightfoot† remarks : " The Apostle doth purposely in-

---

* In this chapter I avail myself freely of the labors of Browne in his *Ordo Sæclorum,* § 328. I only wish I had room to quote him word for word.

† See also Wordsworth's New Testament, 1 Pet. iii, 19; 2 Pet. ii, 5–iii, 5.

tend to compare that old world then destroyed, with *the destruction of the Jewish nation shortly coming.*"

The numerous references of the Apostles in their writings to "*these* last times," "*these* last days," and the like,* all have a bearing in the same direction; though, at the present day, we are so far removed from the overwhelming horrors of that lurid sunset of Judaism, that we are slow to appreciate the sense in which such expressions were used by contemporaries. But as Archdeacon Lyall well observes, in a passage quoted by Browne: "Any person who reads the narrative which Josephus has left us of the events which marked the siege of Jerusalem, and weighs the unspeakable greatness of the catastrophe in comparison with any similar event recorded in history, will see that it *stands alone in the annals of mankind*. .... When Tacitus comes to that part of his history in which he has to relate this event, the expression which he uses marks how deep an impression it had made upon his imagination. *Sed quia famosae urbis supremum diem tradituri sumus,* &c. Supremum diem! there was no metaphor in this phrase, the words were literally true."

In the same connection, Browne calls attention to the phrases used by Daniel and other Prophets, in foretelling "the last days" of Jerusalem. "The end thereof shall be *with a flood,*" or "*like the Flood.*" "And even unto extermination and judgment *shall it rain down upon* the desolate," Dan. ix, 26, 27. In several other places are phrases of the same kind.

To this general correspondence between the two periods, and the two great catastrophes, the following special features of this type relation may be added:

* Heb. i, 2; James v, 3; 1 Pet. i, 20; 1 John ii, 18.

They were both periods of "*long-suffering;*" of a flourishing but Godless *civilization;* of *confusion and corruption;* of *preparation,* "the ark," that is the Church, "a-preparing;" of *deliverance,* the "eight" in the ark, the elect "few" in the Church; of *judgment,* the old world and the Jewish dispensation being swept away; of *a new order of things* in place of the old. Moreover, both periods alike, the end of the Adamic and the end of the Levitical terms, are figures of the end of the present dispensation.

Furthermore, each of these eras had its own representative one of those "two witnesses," Enoch and Elijah, who were taken up bodily into heaven. Enoch "the seventh,"* testified to the one generation; Elijah—who is also a "seventh" in the prophetic series, Noah, Abraham, Jacob, Moses, Samuel, David, Elijah—bore a little heeded witness to the other. In the opinion of many, they are both reserved to testify again before the final coming of the Lord. Again, Noah, meaning "comfort," "the eighth† person," the "preacher of righteousness," the living link between the "old" and the "new," is eminently the type of the Son of Man. Once more, each of these eras had its precisely measured term of "long-suffering" or "provocation." In the world before the Flood, it was 120, that is *thrice* 40 years: Gen. vi, 3. In the Levitical æon, there were

---

* Jude, 14. The correspondence between these two, and the wonderful precision of the type, will be seen more clearly in the chapter on the number *Seven*.

† On the mystical force of this number, associated with the *eighth* or *Resurrection* day, and therefore with our Lord, see Wordsworth's New Testament, Luke xxiv, 1; 2 Pet. ii, 5. See also Chapter XII of this "Inquiry."

the "forty years" in the wilderness, wherein they provoked Moses; the "forty years" of Samuel, wherein they provoked the second great prophet, rejecting the heavenly for an earthly kingdom; and finally, the forty years of Apostolic testimony before the fall of Jerusalem, wherein they provoked God to the utmost, and brought upon themselves a swift destruction.

It will be seen, at a later stage of our inquiry, that these correspondences between the two periods are made mathematically exact, by the identity of all the *Numerals* by which each is measured. Not merely the fact that each period endured just 1,656 years, but that Noah's 600 years, with the 120 years of "suspended judgment," and the *Eight* which is the symbol of Noah, and the *Seven* which is the sign of Enoch, and the *Thirteen* and *Sixty-five* which have also appropriate meanings, are all reproduced in the two periods, under analogous circumstances: this, and more of the same kind, will be brought out by a process strictly arithmetical. It will also be seen that each of these parallel periods had not only its "witness" in Enoch and Elijah, but probably its Law and its Lawgiver, its Apostasy and its Schism, and in a very marked way, its mystical term of "Rest."*

But before we come to this, it will be necessary to go on with our chronological dates, and to show somewhat in detail the process by which they are ascertained.

---

* Eden begins the one: Joshua's "rest," the other.

CHAPTER IV.

THE WAY TO ASCERTAIN THE BIBLE DATES.

THE process followed in this inquiry, for ascertaining and summing up the dates in Scripture, is simple and easy in the extreme.* It is merely to set down honestly as they come, and carefully to add up, the terms of patriarchs, judges, and kings of Judah, which extend in a long and connected series from Adam to Arphaxad, and from Arphaxad to the beginning of the Seventy Weeks of Daniel.

For the period which follows, to the Fall of Jerusalem and the final Dispersion of the chosen People, we take the well established dates of ordinary chronology.

But as the terms above mentioned are in a connected series, *the figures that measure them must be taken as they stand;* in other words, they must be regarded as round, complete, or *tabulated* years.

The liberty taken by some, of treating the years of this series sometimes as years current and sometimes as

---

* As some readers may care more for the *results* of this "Inquiry," than for the process, I may here mention that this and the following chapters to the Ninth are merely chronological, an explanation of the way in which the Table is constructed. The Table will be found at the end of Chapter VIII.

complete, renders an exact chronology utterly impossible; it enables each critic, at pleasure, to lengthen or shorten terms, to clip off in one place, or to tack on in another, till there are as many jarring schemes as there are various interpreters.

The same remark applies to the efforts that have been made to cipher supposed lunar into supposed solar years. All such attempts proceed upon an assumption. And the assumption is one which, at bottom, is against the doctrine of Inspiration. For if we really believe that this long, elaborate, and connected series of dates was written under a Divine direction,* and upon a Divine plan, such a belief will make us cautious about altering it even in one iota. If God speaks of "years," He undoubtedly knows what a year is. Though we may be at a loss, therefore, to know whether the years of Scripture are lunar years or solar, whether they are of the same measure with years now or of a quite different measure, still they are doubtless God's years, they are years that He hath measured, and (unless we have definite grounds for doing otherwise) we are bound to take them and compute them precisely as they are given.

Our simple rule, then, with regard to *all the terms of years which come in the connected series*, is to take them as they come, and to add them up in the figures given. *This rule admits of no exception*, unless the

---

* As this may be read by some who are not willing to admit a *plenary* Inspiration, and who may accuse me of a *petitio principii*, I would here remark, that I assume the Inspiration in this place only as an *hypothesis*. In other words, I construe the chronology on *the hypothesis* that it may be inspired, in order to see *whether the result will be such as to bear out* that hypothesis.

Scripture context in any case should intimate an exception.

There are five places, however, in which, respectively, a doubtful phrase, a disputed link, a gap or *undated* term, an overlapping of two reigns, or a seeming discrepancy, causes a difficulty, and gives room in the eyes of critics for differences of opinion.

But it so happens, in *three* of these instances, that *the difficulty is met by the authority of the New Testament;* in *the other two,* the *context* is sufficient to settle the question in dispute.

The sacred chronology, therefore, is as capable of exact determination as any other matter connected with the Scriptures; if we take the inspired writers at their word, and dismiss the miserable idea that they sometimes speak " inadvertently," or " by way of accommodation," it can be determined with the utmost accuracy.

Having thus announced the Rule, it may be necessary to add that *it does not apply to isolated or incidental dates,* which are outside of the regular series, and show no evidence of being recorded in a *tabulated* form.

Thus the reigns of the Kings of Israel are interrupted by obvious gaps. In many of them it is beyond all question that they are *not* tabulated, or given in years complete. They form no unbroken series, and, taken by themselves, can be constructed into no Table. They are manifestly recorded, each one for itself, in a popular way, and of course may be interpreted by years current or complete, as the context may require. They are not given, however, without a purpose. For in one or two places, especially in one critical place, they afford a certain amount of collateral evidence to the correctness of the results obtained from the regular line of Judah.

Upon these principles, then, and in strict observance of the Rule laid down, let us go on and construct the rest of the sacred chronology. In so doing, I shall take up in turn each of the "five points" of difficulty alluded to above, and show as briefly as I can that they are all capable of solution.

CHAPTER V.

THE THIRD AND FOURTH DAYS.

I. From the Flood to the birth of Arphaxad there are just two years; from Arphaxad to the death of Terah, when Abraham was seventy-five years old, 425 years; from this last date to the Covenant of Circumcision, the Destruction of Sodom and the birth of Isaac, 25 years, in all 452 years from the Flood, or 450 years from the birth of Arphaxad. See Gen. xi, 10–32; xii, 4; xvii, 1; xxi, 5.

This is the *third* or Noachic Day. The only doubtful point in it is whether we shall reckon Abram's birth as occurring in the seventy-first year of his father, which might at first sight be inferred from Gen. xi, 26, or seventy-five years before his father's death. Most critics take the latter, and their judgment is in conformity with *the testimony of the New Testament,* in Acts vii, 4; it being expressly there declared that Abram's "father was dead" when Abram entered into Canaan.

II. The next tract of time, covering our *fourth* Day or period, involves the serious difficulty of *a disputed link* in the connection. In Exodus xii, 40, "the sojourning of the children of Israel who dwelt in Egypt" is stated to have been "430 years." But from what epoch is this "sojourning" to be reckoned? Is it from the arrival of Jacob in Egypt, or (as St. Paul implies, Gal. iii, 17) from "the Covenant," which was "confirmed" with "Abraham"?

The Jews, in the time of the Apostles, and in the time of the Septuagint Version, doubtless understood it in the latter sense; and in this sense it has been received by the mass both of Jews and Christians. St. Paul's authority, I think, ought to be decisive of the question. For though it may be said that he spoke carelessly, considering the precise date "a matter of no importance," or that reasoning with Jews he was willing to argue from the stand-point of a prevalent Jewish error, yet there is not the slightest proof of all this, and it is hardly what we should expect from an inspired Apostle. "Faithful in small things, trustworthy in great," is a maxim which no religious teacher can disregard. Besides all which, if St. Paul considered the date "of no importance," why should he have been so exact in mentioning the precise "four hundred and *thirty* years"? Why could he not have said roundly "400 years"? Or, yet once more, why should the Apostle have been so tender of Jewish errors when he was arguing *against* those errors, and when, moreover, he was not speaking to Jews but to his own children in the Faith? In truth, the plea that St. Paul spoke carelessly, or in the spirit of complaisance, is merely a begging of the question; it assumes that he spoke *incorrectly*, which is the very point to be proved. I do not hesitate, therefore, to reject this theory, and, on the authority of the bulk of interpreters, supported by St. Paul, date the 430 years from the epoch of "the Covenant" with "Abraham."

But where is this epoch to be placed? Many have fixed it at the year 75 of Abram's life; but this was before the covenant with *Abraham*, that covenant name being not yet given. Browne prefers the time of the Vision and Promise in Gen. xv. But here again the same objection applies. "Abraham," as yet, *non est*. Besides, *no date is given* in Gen. xv; and to get up one by "conjecture," as Browne does, is (in so important an epoch) utterly inadmissible.

It seems to me that the events related with such solemnity in Gen. xvii–xxi, 5, beginning with the Promise "confirmed" to "Abraham," *then for the first time so called*, ending with the birth and circumcision of "*the seed*" to whom the promise related; and marked in the time between by the crisis of the Abrahamic Day, the judgment upon Sodom; all these events crowded into one great year, *which is emphatically dated* at its beginning and at its close, and which is furthermore distinguished by the solemn reiteration of that weighty phrase, "this set time .... the self-same day," a phrase afterward repeated with like solemnity *in connection with the Exodus:** all this, I say, seems to constitute an epoch unparalleled and unapproached by any other claimant.

Adopting this date, then, as the starting point, we have for our *fourth* Day, from the covenant with Abraham to the Exodus from Egypt, precisely 430 years.

* Gen. xvii, 21, 23, 26; xxi, 2, 4; Exod. xii, 17, 18, 41.

CHAPTER VI.

FIFTH DAY—THE JUDGES.

The fifth Day is divisible into two great terms, that of the Judges and that of the Kings. The era of the Judges, which we take up first, is given us in three forms, one of which is seemingly at variance with the others.

First, in the Book of Judges and the first Book of Samuel, there is a series of terms in detail,* which may be summed up as follows: the 40 years in the Wilderness; the *undated* term of Joshua's "rest;" 390 years

---

* It seems hardly worth while to swell the bulk of a work like this by giving all these details, especially as (after all) the sum of them cannot be made out *certainly* without the aid of St. Paul. The reader, with Bible in hand, can easily pick them out for himself. I may call the reader's attention, however, to one of the first of the "symmetries" which occur all along. There are *six* Servitudes, and *twelve* Judges or Heroes, Abimelech the murderer and usurper not being reckoned of course in this last category. Samson, the great type of the Resurrection—as will be shown further on—is the *twelfth* in the series. It may also be necessary to caution the reader that Eli, the high-priest, is contemporary with the Philistine oppression, which is also the case with Samson. The dates begin with Judges iii, 8, and continue to Judg. xiii, 1; xvi, 23, and 1 Sam. vi, 1, 13; vii, 2.

of Judges and Servitudes, to the end of the Philistine oppression; an undated period of Samuel and Saul.

Secondly, St. Paul, in Acts xiii, 18–21, sums up the same period as follows: 40 years of the Wilderness; 450 years of Joshua and the Judges; 40 years of Samuel and Saul. In this, he evidently allows 60 years for "Joshua and the Elders who outlived Joshua."

Thirdly, the first Book of Kings, vi, 1, reckons the whole term "after the children of Israel were come out of the land of Egypt," to the fourth year of Solomon, as 480 years. This reckoning obviously dates, not from the beginning, but from the end of the Exodus. On the other hand, it includes 40 years of David and 3 years of Solomon, which are not included in the other two accounts. It covers a term, therefore, which *ought* to be three years longer than the period summed up by the 530 years of St. Paul. In other words, there is a discrepancy of 53 years. How do we account for it?

It may be, that "the *undated* term" of Joshua and the elders, being the promised "rest" under Joshua, and being typical* of that "rest" which "remaineth to the people of God," was *purposely* left without a date by the inspired writer. At all events, though so often and so significantly mentioned,† the period is left vague: here, as in the "rest" in Eden (another type of the Lord's Day), there is a mysterious blank in the Chronology.

Such being the case, the period could be brought into a connected Table only in one of two ways. Either it could be *estimated*, according to such *data* as are fur-

---

* Heb. iv, 9.

† Deut. xii, 9, 10; xxv, 19; Josh. i, 15; xiv, 15; xxi, 44; xxii, 4; xxiii, 1.

nished, or else *expressed by some symbolical figure*, for example, the number "Seven," which is the well known type of "Rest." This latter course would seem* to have been adopted in 1 Kings vi, 1. At all events, if we put 7 for that blank period, and add 390 for the Judges, and 40 for Samuel and Saul, and 40 for David, and the 3 years which had elapsed of Solomon's reign, we get precisely 480 years " after the children of Israel were come out of the land of Egypt; " that is, after the Exodus had been *completed* by the crossing of the Jordan.

St. Paul may have followed the other alternative, and for the mystical 7 may have put in a *probable* or *estimated* † 60. Browne shows satisfactorily that the term of sixty years would fairly cover, and not more than fairly cover, the interval in question.

But however this may be: whether our attempt to harmonize St. Paul and 1 Kings be successful or not, the present inquiry goes on the principle of accepting the New Testament as the *authoritative interpreter* of doubtful places in the Old. For even if it be true, as Dr. Jarvis alleges, that St. Paul spoke merely in compliance with a prevalent Jewish notion, yet the existence of such a notion among a people so jealous of the letter of Scripture as the Pharisees were, shows either

---

* The probability will appear much stronger when we come to examine into the subject of mystical numbers.

† As "Sixty," however, has also a mystic meaning, implying "imperfection" or "expectancy," I am not sure that St. Paul may not have employed it as a symbol of the truth conveyed in Heb. iii and iv, *namely*, that Joshua's "Rest" was only a promise, or an "expectancy" of that true rest that "remaineth to the people of God."

that the passage in 1 Kings did not read *then* as it does now, or else that it was interpreted in some sense which brought it into harmony with the other Scriptures.

At all events, therefore, I adhere to the reckoning of St. Paul, and define the term from Exodus to David as 40 and 450 and 40 years. This brings us to A. M. 3068.

CHAPTER VII.

FIFTH DAY—THE KINGS.

The remainder of our fifth Period, from David to the Captivity, seems to require adjustment in one place only. For all the reigns in the line of Judah are summed up with precision, and in regular succession, except in the case of Jehoram the son of Jehoshaphat. Of him it is expressly said, that "in the fifth year of Joram the son of Ahab, king of Israel, *Jehoshaphat being then king of Judah*, Jehoram, the son of Jehoshaphat, king of Judah, began to reign . . . . . and he reigned eight years in Jerusalem,"—2 Kings viii, 16. It would seem, therefore, that in this case a part of Jehoram's eight years overlapped the reign of his father: and, if so, a deduction will be needed on that account.

The collateral *data* with regard to the kings of Israel, which happen to be particularly abundant just in this critical place, enable us to determine the amount of the deduction needed.

But, to apply these *data* with absolute security, it will be advisable to reckon the reigns both downward from David to the Captivity, and upward from the Captivity to David. We begin, therefore, with fixing the date of the Captivity.

The prophet Daniel informs us, chap. i, 1, that "in the third year of Jehoiakim, king of Judah," Nebuchadnezzar besieged Jerusalem, took it, and carried captive (among others) certain "children of the king's seed;" which "children," after *three years* of training, ver. 5, 8, stood before the king in the *second* year of Nebuchadnezzar: chap. ii, 1, 14. In addition to this, the prophet Jeremiah informs us, chap. xxv, 1, that "the *fourth* year of Jehoiakim" was "the *first* year of Nebuchadnezzar."

Bearing in mind that the Jews reckoned their year from Nisan—say, *March*—and the Babylonians from *January*, we find the above dates to be perfectly harmonious.

Jehoiakim's fourth year, beginning in March, would lie 10 months before and 2 months after the beginning of Nebuchadnezzar's first year. His third year would begin 22 months before Nebuchadnezzar's first, 34 months before his second, and 46 months before *the end* of his second. Thus, supposing Jerusalem to have been taken in the spring or summer of Jehoiakim's third year, there would be ample time for the three years' training of the captive "children;" and also, Jehoiakim's fourth year would synchronize in part with the first of Nebuchadnezzar.

Now the date of Nebuchadnezzar (as is well ascertained from profane Chronology) is the year 604 before the Vulgar Era. Then, the Capture of Jerusalem will be the year 606 B. V. E., in the third year, that is, after two complete years of King Jehoiakim's reign.

This result is confirmed by *all* the other *data*. For example, Jehoiakim (being restored) reigns 11 years in all; and his successor Jehoiachin, or Coniah, after 3 months, is taken by "the servants of Nebuchadnezzar" in the eighth year (7 years complete) of the latter's reign: 2 Kings xxiii, 36; xxiv, 8, 12. Subtract 11 from 608, the first year of Jehoiakim, and 7 from 604, the first of Nebuchadnezzar, and we get in either case the same result, 597 B. V. E. So again: Zedekiah, the successor of Coniah, reigns 11 years; Jerusalem and the Temple are destroyed in the nineteenth year (18 years complete) of Nebuchadnezzar: 2 Kings xxiv, 18; xxv, 8. Subtract 11 from 597, or 18 from 604, and we get in either case the same result, namely 586 B. V. E., the date of the Destruction of the Temple.

It is said in one place, however, 2 Kings xxv, 2, that this last event happened in the eleventh (10 years complete) of Zedekiah. The seeming discrepancy is removed by observing, 2 Chron. xxxvi, 10, that Coniah's 3 months lasted "till *the year was expired;*" and so, in a tabulated account, would reckon as a full year. Thus Zedekiah's reign, including the brief term of Coniah, would reckon 11 years: excluding that term, it would be only 10 years. In either case, there are 11 years complete from Jehoiakim to the end of Zedekiah.

I have dwelt, perhaps tediously, on this, because Browne and some others, setting aside the plain testimony of Daniel, Kings, and Chronicles, and *assuming* the year mentioned in Jeremiah xxv, 1, to have been the year of the first capture of the city, have involved the subject in a tangle from which they escape only by supposing *two* different epochs for Nebuchadnezzar, by changing complete into current years at pleasure, and by rejecting several of the dates given as "manifestly corrupt."

But the prophecy in Jeremiah xxv, 8–11, plainly

foretells an invasion which should "utterly destroy" the city and "make the whole land a desolation and an astonishment." This does not apply to the *first capture* of Jerusalem, for that resulted in little damage either to the city or the land. A few captives were carried to Babylon; but Jehoiakim was reinstated immediately (2 Kings xxiv, 1) and became the "servant" of the king of Babylon. Afterward he rebelled. *Then* "the Lord sent against him bands of the Chaldees," &c. (compare 2 Kings xxiv, 2–4, and Jeremiah xxv, 8)—"and sent them against Jerusalem, *to destroy it, according to the word of the Lord, which He spake by His servants the prophets.*" It is perfectly plain, therefore, that the series of prophecies which were uttered in Jehoiakim's fourth year, and in his fifth, Jer. xxxvi, 9, were subsequent to the first capture of the city, and were occasioned by the king's perseverance in wickedness and insolence *after* so solemn a warning.

Having thus fixed the Captivity where Daniel has placed it, in the third year of Jehoiakim, we add up the reigns of the Kings of Judah from David to that date, and find them to amount to 453 years. But two reigns, as we have said, overlap one another. How much is to be deducted on that account? A careful comparison of the dates in the two lines of Judah and Israel proves it to be just three years.

To help the reader to test this point for himself, I annex a synchronical Table. A brief explanation of that portion of it which bears on our present subject will sufficiently illustrate the principle on which it has been constructed.

As I have said, we reckon the reigns of Judah as years complete. With the collateral dates, we take that liberty which is always granted with years *not tabulated*, accounting them current or complete as necessity may require.

Starting, then, with the first year of Rehoboam and Jeroboam, which is 80 years after the first of David, A. M. 3148, we add 17 years for Rehoboam, 3 for Abijam, and 41 for Asa, and so come to the first year of Jehoshaphat, A. M. 3209. So far the two, checking each other in some ten points, synchronize sufficiently, by counting the years of Israel as years current, and by remembering that Jeroboam's line probably dated from the eighth* month, while the other reckoned from the first month, or March.

But Jehoshaphat began to reign in " Ahab's fourth year:" and Ahab reigning " 22 years," was succeeded by Ahaziah in " Jehoshaphat's seventeenth year." How is this possible? Only in one way. By looking back a little, we find that Ahab began to reign in Asa's thirty-eighth year, 4 years before the first of Jehoshaphat, if we reckon by tabulated years: but he may have begun late in that year, so that the actual time he had reigned may have been less than· 4 years. The same may be true of Jehoshaphat's " seventeenth year." The phrase, in all probability, is popular, not scientific. It may denote merely the time that had elapsed since Jehoshaphat had come to the throne, not the time that would be credited to him in a chronological Table. For the reader will bear in mind that a *Table* always assumes a fixed day as the starting-point of each reign: so that, though the reign may commence actually the last month in the year, yet all the months preceding are counted in with it. The actual length of a reign,

* 1 Kings xii, 32, 33.

therefore, may (in an extreme case) be more than eleven months less than its tabulated length.

Thus, assuming March to be the starting-point of the regal year, suppose further that Jehoshaphat began to reign in February A. M. 3209. The month thus preceding the starting-point would count chronologically as the first year of his reign. Before his first actual year expired, he would be nearly at the end of his second tabulated year. In the same way his seventeenth actual year would extend eleven months into what would be called (scientifically) his eighteenth year.

Now, we have not the shadow of a reason for believing *any* of the dates in Kings and Chronicles to be in tabulated form, save only *those which sum up the reigns in the regular series*. We may therefore assume the contrary wherever the synchronism requires it. This being granted, we can easily reconcile the dates in the case before us.

Ahab began to reign in the thirty-eighth year of Asa, 3205: he reigned 22 years, which (according as we take them for years current or complete) will bring us to 3226 or 3227.

In the other line, Jehoshaphat began to reign, 3209: in his "seventeenth year," which (as we have shown) *may* mean either 17 or 16 when reduced to tabulated form, Ahab died and Ahaziah succeeded. This brings us to 3225, at the lowest, or 3226, at the highest reckoning.

Thus three dates are furnished, 3225, 3226, 3227, from which we select the middle one, because it synchronizes perfectly the two lines of kings.

Again, Ahaziah reigned 2 years—years current as

the context plainly shows—and in "the eighteenth year of Jehoshaphat," i. e., the nineteenth tabulated year or 18 years complete, Joram came to the throne of Israel. This gives us the year 3227. In "the fifth year" of this Joram, 3231, Jehoram began to reign over Judah, *Jehoshaphat his father being still alive,* and reigned 8 years, which brings us to 3239.

But this last date is said to be "the twelfth of Joram, king of Israel," 2 Kings viii, 25, who began (as we have seen) in 3227. If we take "the twelfth" as meaning "the twelfth actual," and equivalent to 12 years in the Table, the synchronism comes out to a nicety, and brings us to the end of Jehoram, as before, A. M. 3239.

Thus, without sacrificing one iota of the principle that the sums of reigns in *the regular line* must be in years complete, we untie the hardest knot that occurs in the whole series. At the same time we prove, what the context led us to suspect, that *Jehoram's reign overlapped that of his father by just three years.* This conclusion is confirmed by the result of the very different process pursued by Browne. For, to effect a synchronism, he also is obliged *to sacrifice three years* in the line of Judah. Only, instead of sacrificing them *where the Scripture intimates* an overlapping of reigns, he adopts the arbitrary expedient of counting three of the reigns of Judah by years current. And even with this help, he falls short of a true synchronism. To approximate to it, he rejects two of the dates—the seventeenth and eighteenth of Jehoshaphat—as "evidently corrupt" —a sorry shift in all cases, but especially so when the "corruption" is by no means "evident."

We obtain a perfect confirmation of the conclusion

we have arrived at, by reversing our process and counting *upward* from the year of the Captivity. Assuming this to be 606 B. V. E., we add 2 years for Jehoiakim, and 277 for the other reigns up to the time of Ahaziah, the successor of Jehoram. This gives us for his date 885 B. V. E. But he came to the throne in the twelfth year of Joram king of Israel. The date of the latter, then, must be 897 or (at the lowest) 896 B. V. E. But he was preceded, 1 year before, by Ahaziah of Israel in the eighteenth of Jehoshaphat of Judah: this gives us 898 or 897 B. V. E. Ahaziah again was preceded by Ahab, 22 years before, in the thirty-eighth of Asa: this gives us at most 920, at least 918 B. V. E. The parallel line of Judah determines it with certainty as 919 B. V. E. But Jehoshaphat, coming 4 years later according to the *data* in the line of Judah, or according to the other line in the fourth year of Ahab, must have begun his reign in 917 at the highest, or 914 at the lowest, or (if we adopt the surer numbers of the line of Judah) in 915 B. V. E.

We have, then, 915 for Jehoshaphat, and 885 for Ahaziah, an interval of just 30 years for the two reigns of Jehoshaphat and Jehoram. But these reigns are together 25 plus 8, or 33 years. Therefore they must have overlapped one another by the space of 3 years. *Quod erat demonstrandum.*

The proof if necessary, might be rendered more rigid still. But it seems unnecessary. We conclude, therefore, by summing up the whole period, which is 40 and 450 years for the Judges, as we have seen in the preceding chapter, and 40 and 450 years for the Kings, as determined in this chapter: in all, there are two terms of "seventy weeks of years," or twice 490, from the Exodus to the Captivity.

CHAPTER VIII.

THE CHRONOLOGY OF THE SIXTH DAY.

The last step in our progress presents no difficulty, most of the dates being fixed in ordinary history.

The Temple, as we have seen, was destroyed twenty years after the beginning of the Captivity, 586 B. V. E.

Fifty years later comes the famous decree of Cyrus, restoring the captives to their sacred land, which brings us to 536 B. V. E. This is the end of the "seventy years" of Jeremiah.

Twenty years later still, after many vexatious delays, the Temple is rebuilt and rededicated, Ezra vi, 15, "in the sixth year of King Darius;" which, as Dr. Jarvis's tables show,* is the year 516 B. V. E.

But here Dr. Jarvis, on the very improbable ground that Ezra, though born in Babylon and bred in the Babylonish court, measured the reign of Darius by the Jewish calendar, sets aside the plain historical date, and ciphers the "sixth year" of Darius into the seventh year. Browne, by a bolder stretch, ciphers the same date into the ninth year of Darius. Hence Jarvis makes the date 515, Browne 513, B. V. E.

---

* Jarvis's *Introduction*, p. 128, and *Church of the Redeemed*, p. 273. The era of Nabonassar, which is the principal authority for the dates of the kings of Babylon, is carefully adjusted to the Julian calendar by Dr. Jarvis and others.

This is done in both cases with a view to adjust the date to certain inferences of an extremely doubtful kind, and with regard to which the two writers are anything but agreed, from obscure passages in Scripture. Were I to take the same liberty, my "inference" might differ from both of theirs, and the plain date given by Ezra might have to be twisted once more into another shape. In such cases the only rule is to adhere to the exact words of Scripture.

The next important epoch, as is generally admitted by chronologists, is the year 459 B. V. E. : the year in which Artaxerxes put forth his memorable decree *to build the walls of Jerusalem, and to restore to the utmost its polity.* This is the decree which accords most fully with the language of Daniel's prophecy,* and is commonly received as the beginning of the "seventy weeks." To the solid arguments which have been given by Jarvis, Browne, and others, in favor of this opinion, our table will add a very singular and beautiful confirmation. For it will be found that the year in question is *introduced* by marked periods of seventy and seventy and seventy-seven years: while the progress of the "seventy weeks" is *emphasized* in several places by an exact coincidence with well-known epochs of history.

The Incarnation is variously calculated at the seventh, the sixth, the fifth, or the fourth year, before the Vulgar Era. I assume the sixth merely as a matter of convenience: for with regard to this date, the more I have examined into the question the more I have been convinced that it is involved (and *purposely*, I

---

* Compare Dan. ix. 25, and Ezra vii.

venture to think) in a haze which is not likely to be cleared away.

The year of the Passion is calculated by Dr. Jarvis as the year 28 of the Vulgar Era. This date accords so exactly with certain *symmetrical periods* which run through the sacred chronology, that I prefer it to the year 29 of Browne's calculation, which is the next most probable estimate.

Not long after the Passion and Ascension, the Jews began to " vex " the growing Church, and Stephen won the first crown of martyrdom. This is commonly placed in the year 30 of the Vulgar Era. The year 31 is the end of the " seventy weeks " of Daniel, and was probably marked by the conversion of Cornelius and the Gospel preached to the Gentiles.

The *forty* years that follow are the last probation of the Jews, and their last " provocation." In the year 70 the Temple was destroyed by Titus, and the Levitical economy came to an end.

Sixty-five years later, which, as we shall see, is a term not less remarkable than the " forty years," Jerusalem was a second time destroyed, by Hadrian, and the circumcised seed of Abraham were forbidden thenceforth to enter the city any more. This was in consequence of the terrible rebellion of Bar Cochbas, " the son of a star," the Antichrist of that period, who, for three and a half years, or " forty-two months," raged furiously against the Christians.

These, with a few other dates of prominent events, taken from the received chronologies, will mark the chief points of the " times and seasons," and bring the sacred chronology to a close.

For the convenience of the reader, I have thrown them all together into the form of a regular Table.

SYNCHRONISM OF ISRAEL AND JUDAH.

		Judah.	B.V.E.	Israel.		
	Rehoboam (March)	17	976	976	976-5	22	Jeroboam (October).
	Abijam	3	959	959	959-8	....	———— 18.
	Asa	41	956	956	956-5	....	———— 20.
2	————	....	....	955	955-4	2	Nadab.
3	————	....	....	954	954-3	24	Baasha.
26	————	....	....	931	931-0	2	Elah.
27	————	....	....	930	930-29	0	Zimri (not counted).
31	————	....	....	926	......	12	Omri (dates from Zimri's year).
38	————	....	....	919	919-8	22	Ahab.
	Jehoshaphat	25	915	915	916-5	....	———— 4.
17 (18)	————	....	899-8	898	898-7	2	Ahaziah.
18 (19)	————	....	898-7	897	897-6	12	Joram (Translation of Elijah).
	Jehoram	8 {	890 === 893	893	893-2 === 893-2	}*	———— 5.
							* (The lower dates computed *up* from 606).
	Ahaziah	1	885	885	886-5	....	———— 12 (2 Kings viii, 25).
	Athaliah	6	884	884	885-4	28	Jehu.
	Jehoash	40	878	878	879-8	....	———— 7.
23	————	....	856	856	857-6	17	Jehoahaz.
37 (38)	————	....	842-1	841	841-0	16	Joash.
	Amaziah	29	838	838	840-38	....	Joash 2.
15	————	....	824	824	825-4	41	Jeroboam II.
	Uzziah	52	809	809	......	....	Interregnum.
38	————	....	......	772	......	....	Zechariah (6 months).
39	————	....	......	771	771	10	Shallum, Menahem.
50	————	....	......	760	761-0	2	Pekahiah.
52	————	....	......	758	759-8	20	Pekah.
	Jotham	16	757	757	758-7	....	Pekah 2.
	Ahaz	16	741	741	742-1	....	Pekah 17.
12 (13)	————	....	730-29	729	729	9	Interregnum. Hoshea.
	Hezekiah	29	725	......	727-6	....	———— 3 (4).
4	————	....	722	722	723-2	....	———— 7.
6	————	....	720	720	721-0	....	———— 9. Captivity of Israel.
	Manasseh	55	696	......	......	....	
	Amon	2	641	......	......	....	
	Josiah	31	639	......	......	....	
13	————	....	627	......	......	....	Prophet Jeremiah (Jer. xxv, 3).
	Jehoahaz (3 months)	0	608	......	......	....	
	Jehoiakim	11	608	......	......	....	
3	————	....	606	606	......	....	Captivity begins.
4	————	....	605	605	605-4	....	Nebuchadnezzar 1.
5	————	....	604	604	604-3	....	———— 1.
	Coniah (3 months)	....	597	597	597-6	....	———— 8.
	Zedekiah	11	586	586	586-5	....	———— 19. Jerusalem and Temple destroyed.

NOTE.—To synchronize the reigns, the years of Israel are reckoned, with a few exceptions, as years current.

SACRED CHRONOLOGY.

A. M.	B. V. E.	Terms of years.	Prominent events.
0	4124		
0	4124		First Judgment: Expulsion from Eden.
987	3137	1,656 years.	Enoch translated.
1056	3068		Noah born.
1536	2588		The Flood announced.
1656	2468	600 y. / 120	The Second Judgment: The Flood.
1658	2466	12 y.	Arphaxad born.
2083	2041	450 y.	Call of Abram.
2108	2016		Third Judgment: Destruction of Sodom: Covenant with Abraham.
2538	1586	430 y.	Fourth Judgment: Pharaoh overthrown: The Exodus, and Eisodus.
2578	1546	490 y. / 40	
2584	1540	40	The Rest of Joshua or Exodus completed.
3028	1096	1,000 years.	Samuel and the Day of Mizpeh.
3068	1056		David.
3108	1016		Solomon.
3118	1006	490 years.	Temple dedicated.
3148	976		Rehoboam and Jeroboam: The Schism.
3404	720		Captivity of Israel.
3497	627		Jeremiah begins to prophesy.
3518	606	70 y. / 390 y. / 40 y. / 490 y.	Fifth Judgment: Babylonish captivity.
3538	586		Jerusalem and Temple destroyed.
3588	536	1,000 years.	Decree of Cyrus.
3608	516	70 y. / 77 y. / 7 w.	Temple restored.
3665	459		Decree of Artaxerxes: Beginning of 70 "Weeks."
3714	410	62 w. / 42 / 21	End of the Prophet Malachi: Vision sealed.
3812	312	70 weeks. / 165 w. / 60 / 44	Era of the Seleucidæ.
3959	165		Temple purified by Judas Maccabæus.
3973	151	490 years.	Asmonæan dynasty.
4086	38	656 years.	Herod the Great.
4118	6		The Incarnation.
4120	4		Death of Herod: The Coming out of Egypt.
4124	0		Vulgar Era.
4148	24		John the Baptist.
4149	25		Baptism of our Lord.
4152	28		The Passion and Resurrection.
4154	30		Martyrdom of St. Stephen.
4155	31	40 y.	Conversion of Cornelius.
4187	63		Beginning of the Judaic War.
4194	70		Sixth Judgment: Destruction of Jerusalem and the Temple.
4256	132	65 y. / 490 y.	Insurrection of Bar Cochbas.
4259	135		Final Dispersion of the Jews: Jerusalem destroyed by Hadrian.
4746	622		Hegira, or Mohammedan Era.

CHAPTER IX.

SYMMETRIES OF NOAH'S DAY.

AND now we will bring together some of the more obvious of the "parallelisms," or symmetrical terms of years, revealed in the chronological table.

The equal length of the period before the flood, and of that which measures the duration of the Levitical economy, has been already noticed. It has also been observed, that even the 120 years term of "suspended judgment" finds its anti-type in the thrice 40 years of "provocation" which occur in the history of the Jews.

A closer examination of their later history shows a parallel still more exact, in the well-known date of the contest between Pompey and Julius Cæsar. For, as we learn from Josephus, this was a turning point in the tide of Jewish affairs.* About the year 70 before the Vulgar Era, the country had been thrown into violent commotions by the rivalry of Hyrcanus and Aristobulus. This brought upon both factions the crushing weight of Roman interference. Pompey marched into Judæa, took the city, broke down its walls, and even ventured to intrude into the Holy Place of the Temple.

* See Joseph. *Jewish War*, B. I, ch. vi–ix; Jarvis's *Church of the Redeemed*, Period V, ch. iv; Prideaux's *Connections*, vol. iv.

Judæa was thenceforward treated as a tributary of Rome, a captive country. But no sooner was Pompey gone, than new and more violent disturbances ensued. Gabinius was, therefore, sent to quell the spirit of rebellion. The Jews fought desperately, as was their wont, but were everywhere defeated with prodigious slaughter. Gabinius at length returned to Rome, and was succeeded by Crassus, who pillaged the Temple, stripped it of its gold, and indulged in sacrilege and outrages of every kind. The contumacy of the people was inflamed to madness. Myriads of them were slain. Some thirty thousand were sold as slaves. Altogether, *it was a dark forewarning of that infatuation which at a later period led to the ruin of the sacred city.*

When Cæsar crossed the Rubicon and took possession of Rome, in the year 50 before the Vulgar Era,* a brighter day dawned upon the Jewish nation. Aristobulus, whom Pompey had carried in chains to Rome, was set at liberty. What was better perhaps for the quiet of the people, he was poisoned, soon after his arrival, by the emissaries of Pompey; also, his son Alexander, the most able and valiant of the leaders of rebellion, was put upon his trial by Pompey's faction, and summarily condemned to death. Cæsar's triumph followed not long after. Thus, with their leaders removed, and with a powerful and clement friend at the head of the Roman government, the Jews were simultaneously disarmed and appeased; and as friends rather than subjects of the universal empire, under the firm

---

* See Jarvis's *Introduction*, p. 171, and *Synoptical Table*, pp. 597, 610. The civil war began 4664 of the Julian period; the Vulgar Era is 4714 of the same.

and brilliant rule of Herod the Great, they began a new career of unwonted peace and prosperity.

The year 50, then, was an era as important to the Jews as it proved to the rest of the world. When Cæsar crossed the Rubicon, he bore with him a *reprieve*, as it were, to a nation condemned, and ripe for ruin. It is a remarkable fact that *this epoch is precisely one hundred and twenty years before the final destruction of the Temple.*

And the six hundred years of Noah, or "comfort," have a similar parallel in these "last days" of the Jews. For from the year when comfort came to the Babylonish exiles, in the shape of Cyrus's famous decree, to the year when "the flood" of the last Judaic War "was upon the earth,"—from 536 B. V. E. to A. D. 64,—there is a space of precisely 600 years.

With coincidences so exact in so many points, it may not be amiss to notice also, that the final siege of Jerusalem, beginning about the middle of March, and ending about the middle of August,* continued just five months, an equivalent to the 150 days that the flood endured.

Thus, in every point in which the test of arithmetic can be applied to these twin eras,† their typical relation is found to be complete. "As the days of Noe were, so also (was) the coming of the Son of Man."

It may be added that most of the prominent dates in those "last days" of Jewish history are marvellously in harmony with Daniel's "weeks," and serve to *emphasize* the prophecy in every stage of its fulfilment.

---

* Jarvis, *Church of the Redeemed.*

† Some other points of resemblance will come out in connection with the numbers Seven, Thirteen, Sixty-five, and Six.

Thus the year 410 B. V. E. closed the *first* seven "weeks;" and it was *probably* about that time,—for we have not the means of ascertaining the date to a year,—that "vision and prophecy" were "sealed" with the death of Malachi, and no more prophets appeared till the time of John the Baptist.

A most famous epoch in the East, the starting-point of the well-known "Era of Contracts," or of the Seleucidæ, 312 B. V. E., marks distinctly the close of *the third* seven weeks.

In the year 169 B. V. E., Antiochus Epiphanes, the Syrian Antichrist, began to rage against the people and the Temple of God.* He defiled the Temple by offering swine's flesh, and "in the hundred and forty and fifth year of the kingdom of the Greeks," 167 B. V. E., he "set up the abomination upon the altar, and builded idol altars . . . . on every side." God raised up a deliverer in the person of Judas Maccabæus. In the year 165, the power of the tyrant was broken. Judas having gained a great victory, the Temple was cleansed and re-dedicated, and the walls of the city were restored. This brings us precisely to the close of *the forty-second* † week of Daniel, or of *the sixth* seven weeks.

The end of the *forty-fourth* week, 151 B. V. E., marks the beginning of the Asmonæan (or Maccabee) Dynasty, which continued to the reign of Herod the

---

* Maccabees i-iv. For adjusted tables of the Seleucid and other eras, see Jarvis's "Introduction."

† Considering the emphasis laid by the prophet on the number 42, it is remarkable that the same number is connected with the date of Bar Cochbas, the second Antichrist; for he began in the 42d century A M.

Great, 38 B. V. E., the end of the *sixtieth* week. On the death of Herod, 4 B. V. E., the probable year of the fulfilment of that prophecy, " Out of Egypt have I called My Son," *sixty-five* of those sacred weeks had just expired. Finally, the *seventieth* week, in the middle of which " the sacrifice and oblation " were caused " to cease," by the offering of the One Victim once for all, was occupied by the ministry of John the Baptist, followed by that of our Lord and His Apostles.

For the close of this *seventieth* week a *definite* date is wanted. The year 31 A. D. was probably the time of the conversion of Cornelius, and of the Gospel preached to the Gentiles. This, however, is nothing more than an estimate; hardly enough for an epoch of such importance. A careful study of the *principle* that underlies the sacred chronology, and especially of *the undated terms*, will show that the silence of history is not less significant than its speech. The very fact that the last half-week is " undated," taken in connection with the extreme precision with which history bears witness to the other terms, is an argument that the last " half-week " belongs to a prophecy not yet fulfilled— at least, not perfectly. It is the " forty-two months " of Antichrist; a term quite discernible in the time that Antiochus raged, more exactly seen in the " three and a half years " of Bar Cochbas, but reserved (as was thought by the ancients generally) for a more ample exhibition at the end of the present Day.

This, however, belongs to Prophecy, a subject into which the present work does not profess to enter.

CHAPTER X.

SYMMETRIES OF THE ABRAHAMIC AND OTHER TERMS.

BEFORE proceeding further with the analysis of the chronological table, it will be well, for convenience' sake, to give names to some of the periods with which we shall have to deal.

Thus, the term of years which *introduces* the Covenant with Abraham, the "evening" of Abraham's Day, may be called the *Abrahamic* term. That which follows we will entitle the *Israel-Judah* term. There is a "forty," oftentimes recurring, which (for reasons presently to appear) we will designate as the *Judah* term. Another of "three hundred and ninety," almost as prominent, is marked out by the prophet Ezekiel as the *Israel* or *Ephraim* term. The same name may be given to "sixty-five," a term mentioned by Isaiah, a factor of "three hundred and ninety." Finally, the famous "seventy weeks," or four hundred and ninety, which belongs to the later history of the Jews, may go under the name of the *Jerusalem* term.

There are reasons for these names, which will appear as we go on; in the mean time we may assume them, as a matter of convenience.

To begin then with the longest, or *Jerusalem Term* of years: In the three repetitions of those "seventy weeks," it will be observed that the second reproduces itself, measuring either from David to the Captivity, or from the building to the re-building of the Temple; so that, in reality, there are *four* cycles of 490 years each.

In like manner, the *three* seventies of the Captivity are obvious; from the Captivity to Cyrus, from the destruction of the Temple to its restoration, from Cyrus to Artaxerxes, the time in which "the land was to have her Sabbaths" is thrice repeated, each seventy overlapping the preceding one by just 20 years. Only, in the last instance, which immediately precedes the prophetic "seventy weeks," the seventy is emphasized by the addition of seven. Thus we have seventy, and seventy, and seventy *and seven ;* the final term of suspense being such as to mark the beginning of a new series of years, and at the same time to contain *the two factors* of that series. "Seventy *and* seven" prepares the way for "seventy *times* seven."

But these "seventy sevens" are equivalent to 40 and 450, or 40 and 20 and 430 years. Again this "four hundred and thirty" is explained by the prophet Ezekiel, iv, 4–6, to be 390 for Israel and 40 for Judah; the prophet being commanded to "lie on his right side" three hundred and ninety days for the one, and forty days for the other, "each day for a year." This being the case, it is certainly remarkable that the whole period from the Covenant to the final dispersion—from 2108 to 4259 A. M.—is just five terms of 430 years each.

In the same way with the number that *introduces* the Abrahamic era, the "evening" (we might call it) of Abraham's Day; if we take the whole cycle from the birth of Shem, which was 100 years before the birth of Arphaxad, to the final dispersion of the sacred people,—100 and 450 and 2,016 and 135 years,—we get precisely six periods of 450 years each.

Thus there are *six* Abrahamic terms of 450 years; *five* Israel-Judah terms of 430 years; and *four* of those "seventy-sevens,"..... *determined upon* ...... *the holy City,*" Dan. ix, 24, which are the terms, or the "evenings" of Jerusalem.

Again, the separate existence of the ten tribes, from Jeroboam to the destruction of the Temple, is precisely 390 years. This, divided by six, gives six minor terms or days of 65 years each.

Now the number 65 is associated with Israel by the prophet Isaiah, vii, 8: " Within *threescore and five years* shall Ephraim be broken, that it be not a people;" a prophecy strictly fulfilled, for from the last year of the flourishing reign of Jeroboam II, 785 B. V. E. to 720 B. V. E., the time when Israel was led away captive, there were 65 years of continuous disintegration. This space, moreover, being preceded by the 40 years of dominion under Jeroboam II, predicted by the prophet Jonas, 2 Kings xiv, 25, naturally directs the mind to that other term of 65 years preceded in like manner by a term of 40, which marks the last days of the holy city, and the final dispersion of the nation.

This being observed, we notice the following curious facts in connection with it. From the Covenant to the Schism, there are 1,040 years, just sixteen terms of 65 years each. From the Schism to the beginning of the Judaic War, there is the same space lacking one year; or, to the end of the war, the same with six years added. So, again, from the birth of Abram to the year 30 A. D., the beginning of the final forty and sixty-five, there are 2,145 years, or thirty-three terms of sixty-five years each. Or, yet once more, from the birth of Terah, Abram's father, to 30 A. D., there are 2,275 years, or thirty-five periods of 65 years each. If we add to this the *final* 65, omitting the intermediate 40 which belongs to Judah, we shall have thirty-six terms of 65, or six terms of 390 years each ; that is, six of the larger terms of Israel.

Thus the number 65, and its multiple 390, is a measure not only of Israel as distinct from Judah, but of the entire duration of the Abrahamic cycle.

The "forty years," the sacred term of Judah, is still more conspicuous as an element of "the times and seasons." In the whole Levitical period it occurs, in a marked or "determined" manner, just twelve times: namely, *thrice* as terms of "provocation," Moses, Samuel, the Apostolic age; *thrice* as terms of deliverance and rest, Othniel, Barak, Gideon ; *thrice* as terms of enlarged dominion, David, Solomon, Jeroboam II; *thrice* as terms of humiliation or servitude, Eli,* Jehoash and Jeremiah. Putting all these together, we have just 480 years. Thus, as there were twelve times forty years (1 Kings vi, 1) between the Exodus and the beginning of "the House of the Lord ; " so between the Exodus and the true Temple (John ii, 19) there were twelve sacred terms of 40 years each, making the same sum of 480 years.

Moreover, all these *forties* are connected with the house of Judah, or with Israel and Judah as a united people. The only apparent exception is one that proves the rule. For Jeroboam II, whose forty years we in-

* The term of Eli *synchronizes* with the 40 years of Philistine oppression. For Jehoash, see 2 Chron. xxiv, 23.

clude among the terms of "enlarged dominion," was indeed king of Israel; but in the preceding reigns, both Judah and Israel had been subdued by Hazael, king of Syria, and so had been brought partially under one yoke, 2 Kings xii, 17, 18; xiii, 3, 7, 22. But "the Lord gave *Israel a saviour*, so that *they* went out from under the hand of the Syrians," 2 Kings xiii, 5. Joash began the deliverance, 2 Kings xiii, 25; and not only so, but he vanquished Judah likewise, and "*brake down the wall of Jerusalem,* . . . . . and took all the gold and silver, *and all the vessels that were in the house of the Lord*," 2 Kings xiv, 12–14. Thus, when Jeroboam II, the son of Joash, came to the throne, he found Judah as well as Israel under his hand, and "restored the coast of Israel" to its original and proper bounds, 2 Kings xiv, 25. It is significantly added, xiv, 28, that "he recovered Damascus and Hamath, which belonged to *Judah*, for Israel." "Thus the Lord saved them by the hand of Jeroboam, the son of Joash." His forty years* of "enlarged dominion" was also a term of virtual *union* between the two halves of the divided nation.

In the same way the number 65 is peculiar to Israel, or to Israel with Judah as a solid people. It enters not into 40, or 480, or 490, or any of those multiples of them, which mark the times of Judah and Jerusalem.

The numbers 40 and 65 being thus in so many ways the symbols of Judah and Israel, the whole is confirmed and bound together by the very remarkable fact, that the Abrahamic cycle at its greatest length—from Arphaxad, A. M. 1658, to the dispersion, A. M. 4259—is

* I call it 40 years, and not 41, because the reigns of *Israel*, as the synchronical table shows, are generally given in years current.

2,600, or 65 times 40 years: in other words, *Israel's term multiplied by Judah's.*

Another number remains, which deserves a word of notice. We have observed that the Abrahamic term 450 exceeds the Israel-Judah term 430, by just twenty years. What is the association connected with this "twenty"? By Jewish law, which in this respect is still the law of Christendom, twenty years is the space in which a son is subject to his father: it is the expectant season of life, the time of apprenticeship, the period of preparation. In all the five places where it is given historically in the Old Testament, it has something of the same meaning. Twenty years Jacob served Laban for his wives and cattle; twenty years Israel waited for a deliverer from Jabin the oppressor —Judg. iv, 3; twenty years Samson judged, and *began to deliver*, Israel; twenty years was the ark in Kirjath-jearim; twenty years was Solomon in building "the two houses." Our table reveals three, and perhaps four, other instances. Twenty years Jeremiah prophesied before the capture of Jerusalem; twenty years elapsed between the capture and the destruction; there were twenty years of delay between Cyrus's decree and the restoration of the Temple. In Abraham's history there is a like twenty years not so positively dated. For he entered Canaan twenty-five years before the Covenant of Circumcision. Some time after this—certainly less than ten years,[*] yet after the journey into Egypt, the separation from Lot, and the vic-

---

[*] Gen. xvi, 3. I have objected to Browne's *calculation* of this date, because he uses it as an *epoch*. When used merely as a date by itself, with no others depending on it, the objection does not apply.

tory over the kings,—he had the vision recorded in Gen. xv. It is highly probable then, that between the promise in Gen. xv, and the beginning of its confirmation in Gen. xvii, there was the term of expectancy, the space of twenty years. If so, all the terms of waiting are just *nine*—a number associated (as will be seen in another place) with the name of Abraham. This result is beautiful and suggestive: for "the father of the faithful" is eminently the type of that patient expectancy which "looks for a city," which "seeks a country."

But this brings before us some of those nicer coincidences or parallelisms in numbers, which to be fully appreciated must be subjected to the test of a separate examination.

In the mean time, taking the largest cycle of our Table, the whole æon from the Creation to the Destruction of Jerusalem, the great six Days of Preparation for the Kingdom, we have a period of 4,194 years. Divide this into six equal portions, so as to get the *average* length or "number" of a Day, and we find it to be precisely 699 years. In other words, a Day of Preparation for Christ averages the Preparation for Noah's *plus* the Preparation for Abraham's Day; or, the Preparation for the Baptism by water *plus* the Preparation for the Baptism by fire: Noah being six hundred years old when the Flood came, and Abram ninety-nine years old when the Lord rained fire upon Sodom. On these last numbers there is more to be said in another chapter.

Again, if we assume the Incarnation to have taken place in the sixth year before the Vulgar Era, A. M. 4118, we shall find just 1,000 years to have elapsed since the finishing and Dedication of Solomon's Temple. For this event occurred in the eighth month (October or November). The Incarnation lies between the Annunciation in March and the Nativity in December. A short time, then, before the end of December in the one thousand and sixth year B. V. E., or before the same point in the sixth year B. V. E., it might have been proclaimed by the tongues of Angels, " the Lord is in His Holy Temple, *let all the earth keep silence before Him.*" For in either case, it was a time of universal peace: in the one instance, Solomon, in the other, Augustus, " having rest on every side, with neither adversary nor evil occurrent."

Again, between the Exodus and the Destruction of the City and Temple by Nebuchadnezzar, there is just the same period of one thousand years. This is the only Millennium in the series that synchronizes precisely with one of the great six Days. It is introduced, however, by another beginning before and overlapping it, namely, that which extends from the Covenant with Abraham to the first year of Solomon. Thus three millennial periods, each distinctly marked, and the middle one synchronizing with the Great Day of the Law and Temple and unbroken possession of Canaan, meet together in the peaceful reign of Solomon. The significance of this will appear more fully as we go on with our Inquiry.

There are other coincidences or symmetries entirely in keeping with those here mentioned. I omit them, however, as most of them are of a character to require nice calculation and copious comment of a historical kind. In the present work, I confine myself to such facts as can be verified by the reader* with the least possible trouble.

* I may here observe, that Browne's mistake in assuming a *calculated* date for the covenant with Abraham causes him to miss precisely those parallelisms or symmetries, which bring out *the system* of the sacred chronology. For example, the nice gradation of *four* Jerusalem, *five* Israel-Judah, and *six* Abrahamic terms, does not appear in his table. So also, he misses that remarkable 65 times 40, which measures the whole Arphaxad cycle. Again, that beautiful 699 years, the *average* Day, does not come out. On the other hand, to do full justice to this industrious and ingenious writer, he traces in those periods not affected by his mistake a vast number of minute parallelisms, some of which are very striking, and which he works out (in some cases) to the very day and hour. I have not followed him in these, for the reason mentioned in the text; though, in omitting them, I sacrifice a good deal of the *cumulative* force of the argument for design. With regard to the *third millennial* period in the Table, I dare say it would be better to date it from the last year of Solomon; in which case it would extend to the year of John the Baptist, and introduce the Ministry of our Lord: from 3148 to 4148. This date is more certain than that of the Nativity; the latter being (perhaps *purposely*) involved in a sort of mystic haze. In either case, the result is very beautiful and significant. For in the one case, the term included between the two extreme millenniums is the 10 years of Solomon's early reign, in which he built the House of the Lord: in the other case, it is the entire 40 years of the reign of " the son of David." The *meaning* of these numbers will appear as we go on with our inquiry.

CHAPTER XI.

PRINCIPLES INVOLVED IN THIS INQUIRY.

Our inquiry, thus far, has revealed a most wonderful symmetry in the larger numbers involved in sacred Chronology. In the great cycles and in the small, in the actual periods and in the average, in Judah's terms and in Israel's, in sacred epochs and in profane, we see certain measures recurring with a marked regularity, disclosing a law of *numerical proportions*, not unlike that which modern science has proved in the distances and gravity of the planets, or to that law of "multiple proportions" which in the province of Chemistry has given celebrity to the name of Dalton.

That the force of gravity should diminish "in the ratio of the inverse square of the distance," or that "the squares of the periodic times of the planets are as the cubes of their mean distances from the sun," strikes one at first as a very strange assertion: on second thought, however, we acquiesce in it, because God, we know, is a wise Architect, and why should not He work, like other architects, by certain fixed proportions of weight or measure or number?

In the same way it strikes one oddly, and at first it is not easy to believe, that each chemical substance has its "number" in relation to other substances, and without observance of those numbers no chemical combinations can take place. For example, "*one* of oxygen unites with *two* of hydrogen to make water. Other gases unite in equally simple proportions, and the volume of the resulting compound, if gaseous, bears a simple relation to the sum of the volumes of its ingredients."

Such statements are listened to at first with a smile of incredulity. The idea seems too simple, and yet too ingenious, to be true. That a few ciphers, arrayed in simple or multiple relation, should contain the wondrous laws of light and sound and chemical combinations, nay the motions, gravity, and distances of the spheres; that God, in framing the universe, should have done it in much the same way as when a woman takes her measure of leaven and hides it in three measures of meal: this strikes one as too trivial, and yet too prodigious, for belief. It jars upon our sense of the Divine immensity. It reveals in the Supreme Mind an attention to details, which in some way or other we associate with littleness of character. It seems to make of the Most High an Arithmetician, an Artist, a subtle Handicraftsman, anything rather than that grand and mysterious Abstraction, which bad poetry and worse philosophy have taught us to identify with our notions of the Sublime.

Hence we are startled more or less by the discoveries of science: and the more simple the laws of things are when first discovered, the more apt we are to be startled by them.

And even men of science, or rather a few sciolists who usurp the name, are slow in accepting the natural inference from their own discoveries. Though the world is full of arithmetic, they do not like to think of God as the great Arithmetician. They prefer to conceive of Him as of a Law, a Chance, a Principle of development, or (with the sophist of Aristophanes) a Vortex* or grand Whirl. In the same way, though the world is full of poetry, yet who dares, in these days, to think of God as a Poet? And when we combine the two ideas; when we find everywhere in His works a fancy infinitely luxuriant, bound fast to an arithmetic infinitely exact; when the high hills " hop " and " skip," and the fields " laugh and sing," yet their dancing and laughter are modulated to a Dorian severity of measure: when science itself bears witness to all this; when the telescope and the microscope, " the two witnesses " of science, unite in testimony to the fact that the universe is a Poem—and that, too, not a prose poem moving *pedibus solutis*, but one in which high thoughts

---

* "*Strepsiades. Who gives us rain?* Answer me that!
  Socrates. These (the clouds) give us rain; as straightway I
    will demonstrate;
        *   *   *   *   *
  Streps. But, hark ye me, *who thunders?* Tell me that!
  Socrat. These, these thunder * * *when they collide.*
        *   *   *   *   *
  Streps. And who is he that jowls them thus together but Jove
    himself?
  Socrat. Jove! 'tis not Jove that does it,
But the ethereal *Vortex.*
  Streps. What is he?
I never heard of him; is he not Jove?
Or is Jove put aside, and Vortex crowned
King of Olympus in his state and place?"
                    ARISTOPH. *Clouds* (adapted from Mitchell's translation).

and low alike are tied down to the strict necessities of number and rhyme and rhythm; when, in short, the two great marks of *intellect and personality*, fancy, on the one hand, severe judgment, on the other, are seen distinctly stamped, and in perfect harmony, upon the minutest details of God's works: yet there are men, nay "men of science" they are called, who will not think of Him as an intellectual Person, a King, a Shepherd, a Poet, an Artist, a Man of War, but deem it more "philosophical" to regard Him as a *primum mobile*, a "first cause" of things; a mainspring of a machine, an inexorable blind fate, anything in fact but an actual and Divine Person.

Were such "philosophers" turned out for a while to graze, the very grass (one might suppose) would teach them a better wisdom. They certainly need, like Nebuchadnezzar, to be "wet with the dew of heaven," that like him they may cease to extol gods "which see not, nor hear, nor know," and may learn to praise Him "in whose hand their breath is, and whose are all their ways."

But men of science are not the only sinners in this respect. Religious men, men who read the Bible and believe it to be *God's Word*, are oftentimes besotted with the same idolatry of Chance.

They profess, indeed, to see "wondrous things" in His law. But when we descend from the general to the particular; when we apply to the Scriptures the microscope of a minute analysis; and when, as the legitimate result of this, we find a multitude of *little wonders*, corresponding to the greater ones, and as perfect in their kind: then, the faith of the present day shrinks from the ordeal; we set down such discov-cries as mere "coincidences," or mere "fancy;" we reason that God, like the law,* cares not for little things: in short, the more proof we find of a method in the Scriptures, and of an artist-like "finish" in details, the more inclined we are, like the sciolists in physics, to attribute it all to chance, and to dismiss it from our thoughts.

It was in a very different spirit that the early Church read the Scriptures. The Bible to them was not a book merely; it was a grand zoön, a "living creature," a thing instinct in every part with a mysterious, manifold and superabundant life. And in every part of it they expected to find the evidences of that life. And as a Divine work differs from a human chiefly in those *minutiæ* which lie beneath the surface; as a photograph, for example, painted by the sunbeam, though it be but a dot to the naked eye, will yet reveal to the microscope what no human skill can rival: so, the early Christians argued, it must be with the Divine Word. They confidently expected to see "wondrous things" in it. And the more closely they scrutinized it, the more marks of the supernatural they professed to see therein.

Hence to them the "history" of the Bible was not mere history; its "facts," not mere facts; its "arithmetic," not mere arithmetic. Each word, each letter, each cipher appeared to them transfigured in an atmosphere of the supernatural, the centre of a vast throng of spiritual associations.

And it was in this temper, mainly, that they applied the terms "mystic," "spiritual," or "sacred," to such common-place things as numbers. However we may

* "De minimis non curat lex."

explain it, certain numerals in the Scriptures occur so often in connection with certain classes of ideas, that we are naturally led to associate the one with the other. This is more or less admitted with regard to the numbers *Seven, Twelve, Forty, Seventy,* and it may be a few more. The Fathers were disposed to admit it with regard to many others, *and to see in it the marks of a supernatural design.*

Now the question, whether they were mistaken in their convictions on this subject, cannot be determined in an off-hand way, or on *à priori* grounds. Supposing God to inspire a book, we can no more tell beforehand how he would inspire it, than we could imagine beforehand what sort of a world it would please Him to create. Nor can we judge whether He would stamp upon this book merely the larger features of His handiwork, or would mark it as He has marked His works in nature. On the whole, however, reason would incline us to expect the latter. ' As we know a leaf to be a leaf, or a flower a flower, not from its general appearance merely, *which may be imitated,* but from certain *minute* indications which from their very minuteness no human art can counterfeit, so we might expect in relation to God's Word. It may have marks on it which are absolutely beyond the *possibility* of human imitation. And if there are such marks, may they not be found precisely in those matters where the wisdom of the present day sees "inaccuracies," or "contradictions," or "difficulties" to be explained by new theories of Inspiration?

The present inquiry is undertaken with a view to this point, and is directed to one of the main "difficulties," namely, that which is connected with the Numerals of Scripture. In going on with it, I wish to rid myself, and I trust the reader will rid himself also, of all prejudices and prepossessions. So far, we have seen something *remarkable* in the larger figures connected with Chronology. We have observed in those figures a marvellous symmetry, a strange mutual correspondence, an extraordinary observance of the law of proportions. May it not be the same with the smaller figures of the Scriptures? May there not be among them " a method," a co-relation, a symmetry, analogous to that which we have already observed in the larger numerals?

The question is one of fact: it is only by a patient induction and clear analysis of facts that we can expect to obtain a satisfactory answer.

Precisely as if it were a question concerning the law of gravitation, or the law of multiple proportions in Chemistry, we must lay hold upon the Proteus of variable *phenomena*, and whatever shape they may assume in our hands, we must not let them go till they have answered our questions.

But, it may be asked, How are we to begin our experiments, and on what general principle are we to frame our questions? I answer, We must begin, as in all similar inquiries, by assuming *something*. In order to put proper questions with regard to gravitation, for example, we must of course assume the *possibility* that gravitation exists. In the same way with regard to the present inquiry: All that I assume, and all that I ask the reader to assume, is that there *may be* something extraordinary in the Scripture numerals. This being allowed, the remainder of our course is plain enough. We are to try experiments, wherever there is an opening for experiments: we are fearlessly to put questions wherever the facts are such as to warrant further questions.

To take an extreme case: In that remarkable account, given by St. John,* of the miraculous multiplication of the loaves and fishes, one of the disciples casually remarks, "*Two hundred* penny-worth of bread is *not sufficient.*" Here *a child* might ask, "Why does he say *two hundred* penny-worth?" Of course *a man* would answer, in such a case, that the question is a "childish" one; or, that the disciple said "two hundred," because "two hundred" was the number that *happened* to occur to him. Such would be the answer ordinarily given. Yet we can conceive that a man *might* reason somewhat differently. He might say within himself, "Perhaps this question after all is not so impertinent as it seems. A great philosopher once asked, *Why does an apple fall?* And though any clown in England might have answered the question in a way to satisfy ninety-nine men out of a hundred, yet the sage went on tormenting himself with it and torturing nature, till he elicited the great law that governs the spheres." Reasoning in this way, one might take up the child's question with regard to the "two hundred," and endeavor, on the principle of *simple association of ideas*, to find whether there was anything in the Hebrew mind that would suggest the number "two hundred" in connection with the thought of "insufficiency," rather than the thousands of other numbers that were equally ready at hand.

The question is a nice one, and I do not say that the effort to find an answer to it would lead to any valuable

* John vi, 7.

discovery. It might easily however lead to this much. It might start a train of curious and interesting thoughts, which being once started, might lead on link by link to an excellent summary of the Gospel. Achan's "two hundred shekels" of stolen silver might suggest the "insufficiency" of money; Absalom's "two hundred shekels" weight of hair, the "insufficiency" of strength and beauty; Micah's graven image purchased with "two hundred shekels," the "insufficiency" of false religion; Hezekiah's "two hundred lambs," or Ezra's "two hundred rams," or Solomon's "two hundred pomegranates" and "two hundred targets," or the "two hundred singing men and singing women" of the Temple restored, the insufficiency even of true religion so far as it consists in sacrifices or external glory: and so we might go on with similar associations, till we come to the great question, What *is* sufficient, and find it to be answered in Him who elicited from Philip the very simple remark, "Two hundred penny-worth is not sufficient."

I give this merely to show the way in which inquiry may be *started*. The aim of the Chapters that follow is much more than this. It is, with regard to certain Numerals, *to test the principle involved*, by a rigorous induction as well as by experiments of a crucial character.

But if the inquiry is to be rigorous, we must of course confine ourselves to a few leading Numerals. I select those which are particularly connected with the subject of Chronology.

CHAPTER XII.

THE DOMINICAL NUMBER TESTED.

The great eras of the world before the Flood and of the Levitical dispensation being both of the same length, and both introductory to an era of "new life," may not the number *eight*, the numerical symbol of the idea of the Resurrection, be a measure or factor of the duration of those periods?

The question, like some others which I shall put, may seem at first sight to be a frivolous one: but it is suggested by the number of curious parallels that have already appeared, and I proceed to investigate it as a sort of *extreme test* of the systematic character of those parallels.

One word, however, touching the *meaning* which we assume for this number *eight:* Dr. Wordsworth says, in his notes on the New Testament, "As the number seven is the sabbatical number, or number of rest, in Holy Scripture, so *eight* may be called the *dominical*. Seven is expressive of rest in Christ: *eight* is expressive of *resurrection* to new life and glory in Him." It may be added that this arises from nothing very mystical or recondite, but from the law of *simple association of ideas*. The eighth day is the day of circumcision; it is the great day of the Feast of Tabernacles, which is a type of the Incarnation: above all, it is the day of the Resurrection, "the Lord's Day," of the Church. Also, the name Jesus, if rendered into numerals corresponding to its Greek letters, is 10, 8, 200, 70, 400, 200, which, being added up, is 888, the opposite of the famous* 666, "the number of the Beast." There are other associations of a like description.

Applying the number *eight*, then, to the dates of Noah's day, we find that *six hundred*, Noah's age, is 8 times 75, which last number also is 5 times 15; that *one hundred and twenty*, the term of "suspended judgment," is 8 times 15; that *sixteen hundred and fifty-six*, the age of Noah's world, is 8 times 207. Thus, into all the terms and dates of the cycle of "the eighth person," eight is found to enter as an even factor.

I may add, in passing, though it leads us off a little from our immediate inquiry, that the quotients in these

---

* The attempts of writers on prophecy to fasten this number upon theological opponents has brought much discredit upon the whole subject of sacred numbers. The ridicule is merited, so far as the coincidence of that number with particular names is made *an argument, by itself;* so far, however, as such coincidence harmonizes with *other* signs and proofs, the fact is calculated at least to arrest attention—which is all perhaps that was intended in furnishing us with this number. In the following inquiry I carry out the *principle* suggested by that number, as also by the 888 of the holy name Jesus, *in order to try* whether there is any principle involved in it, or whether the few acknowledged cases of such coincidence of names and numbers are isolated and exceptional. I have no theory on the subject. I am only experimenting, in the spirit of *free* inquiry, with a view to ascertain, if possible, the precise state of the case.

instances have associations in harmony with those ascribed to eight.

Thus *fifteen* is the numerical value of one of the Hebrew abbreviations of the name of the Lord. It is also connected, as will be seen in another place, with the idea of the *second* resurrection. *Seventy-five*, a multiple of fifteen, and the age of Abram when he entered Canaan, has similar associations connected with it. *Two hundred and seven*, also, is one of those numbers to which a special meaning has been given. It *may* signify a "two hundred of insufficiency" followed by a "seven of rest." But we cannot stop, just now, to put this to the proof, our immediate concern being with the number eight.

We have tried, so far, the dates connected with Noah. Let us now try the "number" of his *name:* an experiment suggested by the fact already mentioned, that eight is particularly prominent in the antitype of Noah, the holy name Jesus. Taking, then, the letters of Noah's name according to its *short spelling* in Hebrew—for it may be spelled two ways—we find them to make *fifty-six*, which is 7 times 8; taking the longer spelling, namely, the word that means "comfort," we get *sixty-four*, that is, eight times eight.

This is remarkable in itself: still more remarkable when taken in connection with the facts ascertained by our previous inquiry. Let us try it by a test still more rigorous.

Noah is not the only type of the Resurrection. Isaac, who "in a figure" was raised "from the dead,"[*] partially embodies that great idea, at least in one crisis of his life. Samson, who slew more by his death than

[*] Heb. xi, 19.

he had slain in his life, who at "midnight" came forth from the stronghold of the enemy, *carrying off the gates;* Daniel, delivered from the lions' den; the "three children" from the fiery furnace; Jonah, who came out from the "belly of hell:" all these are more distinctly suggestive of the same idea, and by those who believe in types at all, are regarded as great and manifest types of the risen Saviour. How is it, then, with their Hebrew names? Will they stand the test that we have applied to the name of Noah?

Isaac in Hebrew numerals is 100 and 8 and 100; the resurrection number standing prominently in the midst, as is proper to one who, "in a figure," was raised from the dead.* Samson, that grand and gigantesque type of the Saviour as a warrior, snapping the cords, breaking the bolts, and carrying off the gates of the enemy, and laughing them to scorn, has a particular predominance of the same marked numeral. His name, if we render the final letter by its lesser equivalent in numbers,† is 696, eighty times eight *plus* seven times eight.

Jonah's and Daniel's numbers have each one ele-

---

* Reviewing this part of the "Inquiry" under the light of subsequent investigations, I find that the *quotients* in these instances are not less significant than the principal factors. Thus, Isaac, or 208, divided by 8, gives 26, which is twice 13, the number of schism or apostasy—as will appear in the next chapter. As Isaac begat *two* nations, one of which was rejected, and as Jacob likewise gave life to schismatical Ephraim as well as to Judah, this is appropriate enough. Abram also was the father of Ishmael as well as of Isaac. But the subject is treated more fully in the next chapter.

† The Rabbins used some *final* letters for higher numbers: n, for example, which stands for 50, was (as a final letter) also 700.

ment, which enters into many of the names of the Old Testament saints, and which is so peculiar that it seems proper (where it occurs) to set it off by itself.

It is the number *thirty-one*, which in more ways than one is associated with the ineffable name Jehovah. It is *three*, the sacred triad, multiplied by *ten*, the sign of infinity, with the addition of *one*, the well-known type of unity. Besides which the word EL, a common abbreviation of the name of God, makes thirty and one. Besides which again, *fifteen* and *sixteen* compose that form of the sacred name which the Jews never dare to utter; and separately, each of those numbers spells one of the two abbreviations of that holy name. For this reason the Jews, in the case of 15 and 16, depart from the common rule of rendering numbers by letters; instead of five and ten, or six and ten, which would be the regular way, they prefer to say *nine* and *six*, or *nine* and *seven*. When the number thirty-one, therefore, forms part of any name, it seems proper to set it off as an element by itself.

Doing this in the case of Daniel and Jonah, we have for the former *sixty-four* and *thirty-one*, or 8 times 8, with the Lord's number added; and for the latter *forty* and *thirty-one*, which is 5 times 8 with the same significant addition.

The same applies to the "three children" who came out unharmed from "the burning fiery furnace." Their *Hebrew* names, respectively, end with the sacred *thirty-one*; and contain, besides, the numbers *eight*, *forty*, and *two hundred*, of all which eight is a factor.

This does not apply to their Chaldee names, Shadrach, Meshach, and Abednego. In them I can detect no special significance, and certainly none in connection with the number eight. This is the more striking because it is precisely what we might naturally expect, *supposing that the coincidences above mentioned are really marks of design.*

Similar results may be obtained from an examination of the names of Joseph, Moses, and Joshua. In these, however, the typical reference to the idea of the Resurrection is not so distinctly marked; there are other associations with their names, which are perhaps more prominent. Especially, in the case of Joshua, there is the idea of "rest," the sabbatical idea.

I will merely notice, therefore, that in the case of Moses, who in his fortieth year escaped death by flight, while in his eightieth the Lord met him and was about to slay him, and in his one hundred and twentieth Michael and Satan contended for his body, there is a lively figure of life renewed. The Exodus, moreover, began with him; and this, undoubtedly, is a type of the new life. Yet these things are cast into the shade by his position as the great lawgiver.

His name accords with this mixture of type ideas. But to analyze it at present would be to anticipate some points, which will come in more properly with subsequent investigations. The same remark applies to the names of Joseph and Joshua.

In the mean time, we will go on with the number eight, and try it by other tests.

There are two great feasts of the Jews, which commemorate deliverance from the jaws of death: namely, *the Passover*, which survives in the Christian Easter, and *Purim*, which was instituted in consequence of that great passage from death to life recorded in the Book of Esther.

The word Pascha, in Hébrew, is 80 and 60 and 8; the word Purim is 80 and 6 and 200 and 10 and 40; the eight in both cases being prominent enough as a factor, but particularly so in the latter. For in this instance, three of the letters separately are multiples of eight, and the remaining two are such when added together; while the whole sum is 336, or *eight* times *forty-two*.*

And this is the more striking because the event commemorated in " the days of Purim" is the liveliest "figure" on record of a sudden transition from the shadow of death to the sunshine and joy of resuscitated life.† At one moment, there was " in every province great mourning among the Jews, and fasting, and weeping, and wailing;" at the next, " the Jews had light, and gladness, and joy, and honor; and in every province and every city . . . joy and gladness, a feast and a good day." No wonder, then, " that these days should be remembered and kept throughout every generation, every family, every province, every city; and that these days of Purim should not fail among the Jews, nor the memorial of them perish from their seed." It was a gleam of " the eighth day" upon the darkness of the captivity. And it may be noted here more distinctly than when it was previously alluded to, that " the fifteenth day," which was the " good day" of the feast, has a like significance with the eighth; for

---

* The frequency with which this number comes up in connection with that deadly hostility to God's people which we associate with the name of Antichrist, is well worth noticing; though, from the pressure of other matters, I can only call attention to it in passing.

† Esther iv, 3; viii, 16, 17; ix, 28.

it is the octave of a *second* week, the "second resurrection." Besides which, fifteen is one of the two abbreviations of that ineffable name which covers "the Lord's day." Also, the number is in several places associated with the idea of resurrection. "Fifteen cubits" up, the ark was borne by the flood; Bethany, the place of the resurrection of Lazarus, was "fifteen furlongs" from Jerusalem. The curious reader may easily find other examples.

These are but a few out of a mass of similar facts which lie hid in the Hebrew, that most living of all tongues: a language which (like Ezekiel's mystic "wheels") seems to have a power of going "on its four sides" at once; which in its every syllable and every letter is "full of eyes," beaming with a strange intelligence; which is a marvel, in short, of child like simplicity and spiritual depth.

As to the bearing of such facts on the drift of the present investigation, it may be necessary to observe that types, like other analogies or similitudes, are not to be expected to be *perfect in every particular*. By the law of association of ideas, a law indelibly stamped on the human mind, one image may almost necessarily suggest another, though the points of difference between the two may be even more numerous than the points of resemblance. Thus, when I read the story of Samson, the *annunciation by an angel* to his mother naturally calls up the idea of another and more momentous Annunciation: so also the promise that he should be *a saviour* to Israel; so, again, his title, *Nazarite* or *Nazarene;* so, again, his seeking *a wife among the Gentiles;* so, again, the striking fact that he must be *delivered up* to the heathen *by his own countrymen;*

so, again, the significant declaration that he wrought a greater deliverance *by his death* than by his life; so, once more, that imprisonment in the stronghold of the enemy's power; that barring of the gates and setting of the watch; that sudden rise at midnight—" early in the morning;" that triumphant breaking forth and opening of the gates: to read all this, *without thinking* all the time of its wondrous parallel, would be to me as impossible as it would be to see the broken image of the sky reflected in a troubled sea, without thinking of the *unbroken* sky itself as presented in the blue vault above. The very nature of a type requires that there should be points of difference, points of imperfection. And the same must apply to types as expressed in numbers. Thus, in the name of our Lord, the *eight* is perfect. It is eight hundreds, and eight tens, and eight ones. Nothing could be more striking or complete. In the name of Noah it is not so perfect, but still comes out in a very striking form. It is eight times eight. So, also, in the case of Samson. So, also, in the feast Purim. So, also, but *in a scale of diminution nicely proportioned to the imperfection, obscurity, or mixed nature of the type*, with the other names and characters cited. The uniformity and precision of this result have in them the features of *law* and *design*, as opposed to chance.

It may also be necessary to observe, in relation to these facts, that, taking them *separately*, no one can attach much importance to them. Their force is in their number, their variety, their symmetry and consistency. Even a straw may sometimes tell us which way the wind blows; but when we see innumerable straws turning all in the same direction, the phenomenon is one that is at least worth noting.

Let us proceed to a criterion of a severer nature still.

Of the types and type-characters so far discussed, there are five which have well-defined *dates* in the sacred chronology. Will it prove with them, as it has proved in the case of Noah, that the figures of these dates are divisible by the Resurrection number?

Isaac begat Jacob *five hundred and twelve* years after the flood: which is *eight* times *eight* times *eight*. Joseph, when he delivered his father's family, was probably *forty* years old; which again is a multiple of *eight*. Moses led the people out of Egypt 880 years from the birth of Arphaxad. He began his career at *forty* years of age; he entered fully upon it at *eighty;* he completed it at *one hundred and twenty.* All these again are multiples of *eight*. Samson's death, most probably, is at the close of the first twenty years of the Philistine oppression, 3008 A. M. Daniel's great prophecy,* which predicts the "latter days" of his people, and ends with the waking "from the dust of the earth," is carefully dated "the third year of Cyrus," namely, *seventy-two* years from the beginning of the Captivity. Of these dates, also, *eight* is a factor.

To Jonah no date is given; but the two numbers which are most readily associated with his name,† *forty* and *six-score thousand,* follow what seems to be the prevailing drift, and are both multiples of eight. In this case, moreover, as in the others before it, the quotients which are yielded are worthy of notice.

Thus, in a number of instances and a variety of

* Dan. x–xii.   † Jonah iii. 4; iv. 11.

ways, which, trivial as some of them may seem when taken singly, yet amount in the aggregate to a crucial experiment, we find the number eight to be prominently associated with the idea of the Resurrection, and with those events, and figures, and names, and dates which are *anywise* typical of the Resurrection. That there is a method in all this, and that it is not mere accident, must be kept before us still as an open question, till we have applied similar tests to other sacred numbers.

It may be added, the meanwhile, as a kind of negative criterion of the result of our inquiry, *that, in our Table there are no epochs, or dates, or great cycles of years, into which eight enters as a factor, except* such as are in some way connected with the idea of the Resurrection.

Thus, with regard to the leading dates: If the reader will examine the Table, he will find that Eight will divide without a remainder into 1056, the time of Noah's birth; into 1536, the time when the Flood was announced; into 1656, the time of the Flood; into 3008, the *probable* time of Samson's death; into 3608, the restoration (or resurrection) of the Temple; and finally, into 4152, Dr. Jarvis's estimate of the date of the Passion. These include *all* the dates,* save

---

* Having since had occasion to *add* a few dates to the Table, I find one among them divisible by *eight:* namely, the time when Herod died and "the young child" *condemned to death* by him was "called" back "out of Egypt." This is no exception to the general rule; for the event, and all the ideas connected with it, savor of "new life," "deliverance," restoration, or resurrection. There is another date added more recently, namely that of Bar Cochbas, the peculiarities of which are mentioned further on, Chap. XV.

only one, that we would naturally associate with the idea of the Resurrection. All of these are divisible by Eight. Among all the others, however, *not one is so divisible*. The rule therefore holds, both positively and negatively.

And with regard to the one exception: the Exodus *began* in 2538, and would have been perfected that year, had it not been frustrated by lack of faith among the people. But owing to the lack of faith it was prolonged forty years. At the end of this term the Israelites crossed the Jordan and *began* to take possession of the promised land. Six years later, or just 45 years after the Report of the Spies and the turning back into the wilderness, Josh. xiv, 10, the work was completed, and "the land had rest from war:" Josh. xiv, 15. This gives us the year 2584 for the *completion* of the Exodus: a number which (like the epochs before mentioned) divides evenly by Eight. The seeming exception, therefore, establishes the rule.

As to the leading Terms or Periods: The 480 years between the Exodus and the Temple, or (its mystical equivalent) the twelve terms of 40 years between the Exodus and the beginning of the spiritual "House of God;" the *four* terms of 490 years which cover the Day of Jerusalem; the 1,040, or sixteen times 65 years during which Israel and Judah were one solid people: all these are terms expressive (either in figure or in reality) of the *entire period of preparation* for the Lord. They point distinctly, therefore, to the era of "new life." Accordingly, all these are divisible by Eight, with quotients in each case more or less significant.

But it is not so with the Israel terms, or with the Israel-Judah terms, or even with the Abrahamic terms,

65, 390, 430, 5 times 430, 450, 6 times 450. None of these have Eight as a factor. "Salvation is of the Jews." To the Jews and to Jerusalem the resurrection came. The new Church sprang out of the old. To Israelites as separate from Jews, or even to Abrahamites except as concentrated in Judah, there was no *special* part in the Resurrection. The Gospel was preached to "the Twelve Tribes" as a unit: and it is upon this one stock that the seed of Abraham, whether his seed by blood or his seed by faith only, were *in all cases alike to be ingrafted*.

And, in accordance with this, we are led on to apply another test to the Resurrection number. In the New Testament there happen to be *eleven* figures which we can naturally associate with the general idea of the "new life" and "new world." In Acts i, 14, 15, we have the Church of the Resurrection in its *germ*. "The number of the names together were about a hundred and twenty:" that is, 8 times 15—the Resurrection number multiplied by the number of the "second Resurrection." In Rev. iv, 4, 8; and vii, 3-8; xiv, 1, 20; xx, 2; xxi, 16, 17, we have numbers connected with the same Church in its *completeness*. There are "twenty-four elders," 8 times 3; "four beasts" or "living creatures" with six wings each, 8 times 3; "twelve thousand" for each Tribe, 8 times 15 multiplied by 100; "one hundred and forty and four thousand" for *all* the Tribes, 8 times 8 times 15 times 15 times 10; the same number of "Virgins" following "the Lamb whithersoever He goeth;" "sixteen hundred furlongs," the extent of the wine-press filled by the "ripe grapes of the earth," 8 times 8 times 25; the "thousand years" of "the first Resurrection," 8 times 125; the "twelve thousand cubits" length of the "four-square" city, 8 times fifteen multiplied by 100; the same city in its square, 8 times 8 times 225 thousand; the "hundred and forty and four cubits" of its wall, 8 times 9 times 2: in all which numbers Eight is obviously a principal factor, while the other factors are such as we have already seen to be in harmony with it.

Thus, negatively and positively the rule holds good. Wherever there is a distinct and special pointing to the idea of the Resurrection, whether in dates or other numbers, we may look for the figure Eight as prominent in one form or another. Where there is no such special relation, the figure is not thus found.

I may add, as a final negative test of the severest character, that if we divide the dates in the *second* column of our Table by Eight, there are some fourteen of the figures into which it enters as an even factor, but in no case with any special or consistent meaning.

But the dates in this column reckon from no real epoch. The "Vulgar Era" is purely arbitrary, the Nativity having occurred some six years before it.

The fact, then, that out of two equal rows of numbers, embracing some eighty in all, the one set is divisible by Eight in *fourteen* instances, but *always without significance*, while the other set is divisible in *six cases only*, all of which are associated with one and the same grand idea: this, taken in connection with the further fact that the first set is purely arbitrary, while the other is constructed on Epochs fixed by the Scriptures, is certainly a strong argument against Chance, and for Design, in the structure of the Sacred Chronology.

The force of the argument is increased by the fact, that all the experiments which have been made and the tests which have been applied, have been suggested by the *hypothesis* of a consistent Design. I have uniformly reasoned in this way: *If* the coincidences already proven are real, not casual, *then* similar coincidences will be found in similar cases. Hence I have been led on to try the cases that seemed to be similar.

And it is on this principle that experiments are usually tried, and discoveries made, in the province of physical science.

If, for example, the laws relating to the gravity and distances of the planets be true, then there ought to be a planet between Jupiter and Mars. Accordingly, the telescope is set in that direction. After years of patient watching no planet is found, but an equivalent is discovered in a flock of planetoids or fragments of planets. The reality of "the law" is thereby confirmed. By the same reasoning precisely, the planet Neptune was looked for and at length discovered. A few such inferences, confirmed by actual discoveries, especially if no exceptions arise that cannot be explained, are sufficient to establish any law as "a law of nature."

The number Eight, then, has been tested in a scientific way.* On the same rigorous principle, and by similar tests, let us go on and try a few other numbers.

* For a larger induction, see Appendix B.

CHAPTER XIII.

THE NUMBERS SEVEN, NINE, THIRTEEN.

The reader will bear in mind that our present object is one of inquiry only: an effort to ascertain whether the symmetries observed in the Numerals of the Bible, and more especially in its Chronology, are of a systematic character reducible to rule, or are merely of the nature of odd coincidences.

With this object still in view, let us now take up *Seven*, the sabbatical number.

And first a word may be needed, as to the meaning of the word "sabbatical." Its root idea, undoubtedly, is that of "rest." But the "Sabbath" is not, as the Jews imagined, *a cessation from work:* it is a resting or ceasing from a particular kind of work; a passing from a lower to a higher order of Divine occupation. Six days God labored in preparing the earth for man. On the seventh day he rested from this work, and entered upon one infinitely higher, namely, the care of that master-piece of creation, so "fearfully and wonderfully made," which crowned and summed up the preparatory six days.

So also in history: six days, or ages, God prepared the way for the Son of man. The seventh day that followed was a day of "rest," namely, of rest from the particular work involved in the idea of preparation. It was not to be a rest from work of every kind. On the contrary, as in the siege of Jericho the city was encompassed once only during each of the first six days, but *on the seventh was encompassed seven times*, so in this seventh day of the world and of the Church. It is an age of higher work, of aims more spiritual, and of achievements more wonderful, than any that have gone before. Its conflicts and its weapons are of a more spiritual character. It is, in fact, the age of the Spirit. The Holy Ghost has come with his seven-fold gifts. Eden, with its four-headed river, its tree of knowledge, and its tree of life, is in some sense restored. Such, at all events, is God's gracious purpose. The Christian era is the true "rest" or Sabbath; and though men fail to "enter in," just as the Jews failed in the "rest" of Joshua, yet it is "because of unbelief;" we are slow to realize the wonders by which we are surrounded.

This being considered, it will be easy to understand how it is that the sabbatical number *seven* is also, in Holy Scripture, a symbol of the Spirit. Our seventh age is the day of the Holy Ghost. Our first Comforter, or "Comfort," is gone up on high; but He hath sent another Comforter, "whom the world cannot receive, because it seeth Him not, neither knoweth Him." Moreover, He hath sent Him with "gifts" for men. Not in religion only, but in what are called "the discoveries of science," in the wondrous and ever-growing command of the elements of nature, in the startling revelations of the hidden secrets of the past, we have indications of the presence of the Spirit, with His "gifts," though the age to which that presence is vouchsafed, and which profits by it, takes all the credit to itself, and gives man the glory that is due to God only.

But to return from this digression: *Seven* being the sabbatical number, and consistently with that idea, the number of the Spirit, let us examine it by the same rigid rule which we have applied to the number eight.

As Noah was "the eighth person," Enoch in like manner is declared* to be "the seventh." Has the number seven, then, any particular or marked connection with the name or the dates of Enoch?

As to the name: Henoch is 8, 50, 6, 20; that is, if we add the extremes and means, 28 and 56, or four sevens and eight sevens; or if we add in another way, 14 and 70, two sevens and ten sevens; or if we add all the terms in one sum, 84, which is twelve sevens. The number seven, therefore, is the chief numerical element in the name of Enoch, "the seventh."

As to his date: the year 987 A. M. is the time of his translation, the time when "the Lord took him" to His "rest." Divide this by seven, and it gives a quotient of 141: that is, *perhaps*, 120, the term of "suspended judgment," *plus* 21, the period of three "rests;" or, as 120 is equivalent to three forties, it may be interpreted three "probations" followed by three "rests."

But to go on with the *facts:* the name of Enoch as "the seventh" naturally leads one to inquire why he is so called. The obvious answer is, that he was the seventh from Adam, the seventh in the genealogical series. But if that be the case, may there not be parallel peculiarities in the names and numbers of others of that

* Jude, 14.

series: in Adam, *the first*, which is the number of "unity;" in Enos, *the third*, which is the number of "trinity;" in Mahalaleel, *the fifth*, which is the number of "the Law;" or in Lamech, the immediate predecessor of Noah "the eighth"?

The test, it must be acknowledged, is an extremely severe one, but the success of previous experiments induces one to try it.

To give the result of it in full, would lead us too far off from the number "Seven." It will be enough to remark that in each case it accords with the result of previous experiments. Thus, Mahalaleel being "fifth," and Five being a number associated with the Law and with Moses, we find his name to be 40, 5, 60, 31, which is the *forty* of Judah, the *sixty-five* of Israel, the *thirty-one* of the sacred Name. In this connection it may be mentioned that the name Moses is 345, which is seven *forties* and one *sixty-five*. The name Israel also is 510, that is, three *forties* and six *sixty-fives*, with the *thirty-one* of the sacred Name. The significance of this subtle association among those three names will appear more fully in another place. In the meanwhile, as touching more particularly the number *seven*, the drift of previous inquiries would lead us to expect in Lamech, the immediate predecessor of Noah "the eighth person," some prominent allusion to that numeral which symbolizes the eve of the final resurrection. Nor will the expectation be disappointed. Lamech, we find, is 70 and 500; while his age, or "all his days," is *seven* and *seventy* and *seven hundred* years. What an emphasis this gives to that person named "the eighth," and those "few, that is, eight souls," who passed from the death of the old world gone to its rest, into the new life illumined by the rainbow of promise!

But again: the name of Enoch, the first translated witness, naturally directs the mind to Elijah, the witness of the second grand period, who was in like manner with Enoch caught up into Paradise and no more seen. Will the test which we have applied to Enoch's name and numbers be found to hold good in the case of Elijah?

As to his name: Elijah, spelled in full, is 31, the number of Deity, and 21, three sevens or "rests:" the same element that we observed in the name of Enoch.

As to his dates: the time of his translation was the first year of Joram of Israel,* 3227 A. M. Divide this by seven, and it gives us 461, which is 31, the number of Deity, added to 430, the Israel-Judah number.

Again, the interval of time between the two translations is 2,240 years. Divide this by seven, and it gives 320, which is equal to *eight forties*. Now, if the reader will look back to that list of forties which we have drawn out in Chapter X, he will find that there were *just eight of those mystic terms of forty years*, during the interval in question. Can this coincidence be casual? It seems almost too extraordinary to be real. Yet if we test the matter in another, and totally independent way; if we subtract the *quotient* obtained in Enoch's date from that obtained in Elijah's, namely, 141 from 461, we get precisely the same 320, or eight forties, the mystic measure of the sacred times between the first and second great witnesses!

There is, then, to say the least, a marked association

* Compare 2 Kings i, 17; ii, 1-15; iii, 5, 7, 11.

of the number seven with "the two witnesses," Enoch and Elijah.

As to Elisha, that great prophet to whom Elijah was the forerunner, who inherited a double portion of his spirit, who was so richly and manifoldly typical of the Incarnation, we have no certain dates. His name, however, is the sacred 31 added to 300 and 80, or to 300 and 10 and 70. Now the number 300, being the length of the ark, the term of years that Enoch "walked with God," the number of "men that lapped" in the host of Gideon,* with other associations of like character, seems to be symbolical of the Church of God. We may, therefore, put it apart as a term by itself. So also the 70 and 10 are each significant. So also with 80, the sum of these two numbers.

His term of prophesying began in the first year of Joram of Israel, and continued into, and perhaps through, the reign of Joash. If so, it lasted 72, or 9 times 8 years. But over the life of Elisha there is something of that *veil*, that absence of precise dates and figures, which we observe in the three parallel terms of Adam in Eden, Joshua's "Rest," and the Incarnation or Nativity of our Lord Himself. These four *undated* terms have an obvious relation one to another. The fact that, when so many dates are fixed with such marvellous precision, these four alone should be left in a certain haze, is not among the least of those evidences of design that encounter us at every step.

In the case of Abraham the dates are much more precise, and it is easier to try the principle which is the

---

* The application of this type to "the elect" of God's Church is beautifully made in the Baptismal office of the Jerusalem Liturgy.

object of our inquiry. I confess, however, that I almost shrink from giving all the facts which start out on the application of our tests. But we are engaged in an inquiry. The only honest course, therefore, is to follow whatever paths the course of the inquiry may open before us.

As Enoch is "the seventh" and Noah "the eighth," so Abram would seem to be "the ninth" in the sacred series, both as the next type character after Noah, and as being the ninth in the succession from Arphaxad. Let us apply this number to his name and dates.

His name Abram, "Father of Highness," is 243, or 3 to the fifth power, or *nine* times *nine* times *three*. If we add five to this, the value of the letter inserted for his covenant name Abraham, we get 248, which is *eight* times *thirty-one*, the number of Deity.

We observe, then, in his names a curious combination of *three*, the Trinity number, of *nine*, which (for reasons not necessary to mention) appears to be the number of "paternity," of *five*, the number of "the Law," and of *eight*, the Resurrection number. This I mention only in passing, the meanings which I suggest for these numbers being of a character to *add to the significance* of the facts about to be elicited, but not in any way essential to that significance.

To proceed with the simple facts: if we multiply *three*, which is the prime factor of the original name, by *five*, which was added for the covenant name, the product is *fifteen, the number of cubits that the flood bore up the ark.*

Now, the idea of the ark being started, every experiment is found to lead us in the same direction.

Abraham's great cycle, from Shem to the dispersion, appears from our table to be just six Abrahamic terms of 450 years each, or in all 2,700 years. Divide this by nine, and it gives us 300, *the length of the ark*, as a quotient. Divide the shorter term 450 by nine, and we have 50, which is *the breadth of the ark*. Divide the same by *three*, the third factor of his name, and we get 150, *the number of days the flood* was upon the earth. Divide this last by *five*, which is the numerical value of the letter added to make Abraham, his covenant name, and we get for a quotient 30, *the height* of the ark. Finally, *the cubic measure* of the ark is 450,000: namely, a day of Abraham multiplied by a thousand. Now, as the crisis of Abraham's day is that judgment upon Sodom which we have before spoken of as the "Baptism by Fire," this persistent reference in his name and numbers to the previous "Baptism by Water," and to the ark, the church of God, tried both by fire and by water, and to the name of God, whereby alone we must be saved, and to the Resurrection, by which (as St. Peter says) "baptism doth now save us" —this constant, varied, and most emphatic allusion to one grand and pregnant idea is certainly most remarkable. Were it our object to *invent* a *formula* which should express in numbers the idea of the "father of the faithful," it would be hard to hit upon one more striking or more significant. When we come to the application of our *tests*, we shall find this result to be as beautiful as it now appears to be remarkable.

In the mean time, there is another character as mysterious as Abraham, and historically the father and type of one of the greatest developments of Antichrist.*

* See Forster's *Mohammedanism Unveiled;* which brings out

It is Ishmael, the first-born of Abram's strength, but "the son of the bond-woman;" the offspring of Sarai's impatience, the plague of Sarah's life; the "wild man," and the outcast from "the household of faith," who was yet found out by an angel; the circumcised scoffer at "the child of promise," whom yet "God shall hear;" the loyal rebel, the prayerful infidel, the sensuous saint, the kind-hearted hater of his kind: the type, in short, of a humane inhumanity, of an irreligion that is most religious.

His name, when reduced to numbers, is almost as puzzling as his life and character. It accords with the name his mother gave him, "Whom God shall hear." It is eminently a symbol of the *religious* man. It has the 10 of infinity, the 300 of churchly life, the 40 of probation, the 70 of rest, all crowned by the 31, the sacred number of Deity. Yet, added up, they all make 420, the 42 of Antichrist multiplied by infinity. And this 42 is *seven* times *six:* the heavenly multiplied by the earthly, the number of "the beast" by the number of the sacred rest.

With regard to his dates: Ishmael was *thirteen* years old when circumcised, a number still observed by the Ishmaelites. The critical point of his religious history occurs far down in the "seventh" age, the year 622 of the Vulgar Era, the Hegira of Mohammed. Between this date and that of Ishmael's circumcision, when Abraham was ninety-nine years old, there are precisely 2,639 years. Divide this by 13, and the result is 203, or seven times twenty-nine. The *thirteen*

---

the *spiritual* aspect of Islamite history with singular beauty and truth.

of Ishmael, therefore, is an even factor of the grand epoch of Ishmaelite history.*

As to the meaning of this number, apart from its special connection with the name of Ishmael, there is much to associate it with the idea of revolt, of schism, of apostasy. Its first mention in Scripture brings it out in a certain contrast to *twelve*, which is the symbol of organic unity, national or ecclesiastical. "Twelve years they served Chedorlaomer, and in the *thirteenth* year they *rebelled*." Gen. xiv, 4. A "straw," pointing in the same direction, is found in the fact that "in the days of Peleg the earth was divided," and his brother Joktan became the father of *thirteen* nations. Gen. x, 25–29. But the great fact which gives significance to all such indications is one familiar to most readers of

---

* I may here observe that I have applied this number 13 to the *prophetic* numbers connected with Antichrist. The results are curious, but quite inexplicable. Indeed, I expected nothing different. For prophecy is not intended to lift the veil of the future. So far as any system can be discovered in the use of Scripture numerals, it will be found that the system applies only to the past; for numbers bearing upon the future the key will continue hidden. The scheme of prophecy is evolved only by its fulfilment. *Solvitur ambulando.*

And in this respect I may claim that the present inquiry goes on grounds different from those occupied by the students of prophetic numbers. In their case, the facts that are to test their theories are all in the future. In the present inquiry, everything can be tried by *accurately dated facts.*

While I am about it, I may also notice, that the point above mentioned is *not the only one*, where the sacred chronology links on to Islamite history. Others, even more significant, will be seen farther on. Nothing has struck me more, in this "Inquiry," than the fact that *every point* is established by "*two or three* witnesses."

the Bible: to wit, that while Israel consisted actually of *thirteen* tribes, yet out of eighteen enumerations which occur in the Old and New Testaments they are invariably so numbered as to make only twelve. Generally, Levi is the one omitted; in one place Simeon. In the book of Revelation, however, Dan is left out, and Joseph is inserted in the place of Ephraim. Such regard for the number *twelve*, with such careful avoidance of *thirteen*, is enough in itself to show that some peculiar meaning was attached to each of those numbers.

This is further shown by the numbers of Israel's name, which, taken separately, are the 10 of "infinity," the 300 of "churchly life," the 200 of "insufficiency," and the "one and thirty" of the sacred Name. Taken together, apart from the 31, they make 510, which is the 390 of Ephraim with thrice the 40 of Judah. It has been already noticed that the name Moses contains the same 40 of Judah, along with 65, which is a factor and another form of the Israel or Ephraim number.

But this 65 is *five* times *thirteen*. While the Judah term, therefore, is the Resurrection number multiplied by the five of the law, the Ephraim term is the ominous schism number multiplied by the same.

And now for an experiment based upon *two distinct inferences* from the law that seems to govern these sacred numerals. Having met with a remark in an old writer to the effect that every half millennium seemed to be about the season for a new revelation, or covenant, or something equivalent, but that the writer had been able to discover nothing to support his theory near the end of the *first* five hundred years, it struck me that the name of Mahalaleel might possibly contain indications of something of that sort during his time. Accordingly, I tried his name, with the result already mentioned. I found his name to be typically the same as that of Moses. It then struck me, as a *second inference* from the same premises, that, as Mahalaleel seemed analogous to Moses in other respects, I might also find in his period some indications of the presence of schism or apostasy.

Accordingly, I found that he begat Jared, when he was *sixty-five* years old; and that Jared lived 962 years, which is 74 times the ominous *thirteen*. Furthermore, Enoch lived *sixty-five* years, and begat Methuselah. Three hundred years later, the number of the Church, he was translated; so that all his days were three hundred years and *sixty-five* years. Moreover, he was translated in the year 987, *thirteen* years before the close of the first millennium. So persistent a repetition of the numerals of schism, in connection with the Israel and Judah numbers, would warrant one in suspecting that Enoch, like Elijah, had his Moses; and that he lived in the times of an apostasy similar to that to which Elijah preached; perhaps the apostasy which is mentioned, but not dated, in the sixth chapter of Genesis. The age of the world at Mahalaleel's death, namely, 1,290 years, which is thrice the Israel-Judah number, would seem to point somewhat in the same direction.

A like inference led to a closer examination of another era of division. "In the days of Peleg," a name which means "division," "the earth was divided." In connection with which we find, by counting the names, that Joktan, the brother of Peleg, was the father of *thirteen* tribes. In which connection, again, it is certainly remarkable that Peleg's name in Hebrew is one hundred and *thirteen;* while Joktan's is 819, that is, seven times *thirteen* multiplied by nine,* the symbol of "paternity;" or, as it may be otherwise resolved, *thirteen* times fifty and *thirteen*. This result is obtained by giving the last letter its higher numerical value† as a "*final* letter." If we take it according to its lower value as an ordinary letter, Joktan would spell 10, 100, 9, 50, or 169, which is *thirteen* times *thirteen*. Now, inasmuch as this Joktan broke off from the sacred family of Eber, *and settled in Arabia*, his descendants, like those of Ishmael, became eventually an element of the great Saracen power, and are thus identified with that mighty manifestation of the spirit of Antichrist, the Mohammedan apostasy.

To return now to the more exact inquiry with which this chapter begins, and to apply to the numbers examined in it the same criterions which we have applied to *eight:* we find that the number *seven* is an even factor of the dates already mentioned in connection with it, and of no others in our table whatever, *save only the date of Solomon's reign.*

But what is the type relation of Solomon in sacred

---

* There is much to warrant the idea that *Nine* is associated with the idea of "paternity," but to prove it would require more space than I can give to it just now.

† I find generally, that where the final letter has a higher numerical value, the type meaning is less apt to appear with that, than with the lower and alphabetical value. These higher values, it is probable, are of later and rabbinical invention. In many cases, however, as that of Joktan, the result is not materially affected by the difference.

history? His was a reign of "rest" and peace, "with neither adversary nor evil occurrent," especially chosen for that reason as the season for the building of the "House of God." It is a figure of "the kingdom" of "the Prince of Peace:" a type of the great "seventh day" of the Christian dispensation. The very name Solomon means "rest" or "peace." His number is the 300 of the church, the 70 of rest, the 5 of the law. He was "seven years" in building the House of the Lord: though in building *his own house*, which was afterward so grievously divided, he fell upon the ominous "*thirteen* years."

That seven, therefore, should enter as a factor into the date of Solomon's reign, is entirely in accordance with the results of our previous investigations.

Joshua's time, where we might also expect to find it, is left *undated* in the Scriptures; but, as I had occasion to show in another connection, the term of 480 years, in 1 Kings vi, 1, can be reconciled with the statement of St. Paul, Acts xiii, 20, and with the numbers given in the book of Judges, only by *allowing for* Joshua's "rest" a *mystical* term of seven years. I may also here remark that the other undated term, the life of man in Eden, is likewise associated with the same number of "rest." For the word Eden, in Hebrew numerals, is 70 and 4 and 700; in which the *four*, like the seven, has a marked significance.

It may also be worth noticing, in connection with this number, that, among the three sons of Noah, Japheth is the one who has proved historically the lord of the present era. He "dwells" in the "tabernacles of Shem." To him has fallen the largest share of "the gifts" of the seventh day: he, on the whole, has been the most faithful in their use. Now I can fix on no particular date in connection with Japheth. When I turn to his name, however, and to the names of the nations that sprang from him, in that tenth chapter of Genesis, which is a grand study by itself in this connection, I observe first, that his number is the famous "seventy sevens," the 490 of the sacred people and holy city; secondly, that his immediate descendants are *seven;* thirdly, that from them spring two other groups, the one of *four* and the other of *three*, making in all *seven;* fourthly, that the whole number, including Japheth himself, is the sacred *fifteen*, a number of Deity, and the number of the second Resurrection.

And here it may be noted that the *four* and *three*, which in one of these instances compose the number seven, are what may be called numbers of perfection: *three*, of spiritual or essential, *four*, of material or organic perfection.* The number seven, therefore, may derive its proper meaning in part from them. Also the number twelve is *four* times *three*, essential multiplied by organic perfection, and stands as the symbol of organized fraternity, of national or ecclesiastical brotherhood. For it is to be observed that it is not confined to Israel or to the sacred city. Ishmael, as well as Israel, had his "twelve princes."

And in examining the name of Ham, in the same tenth chapter of Genesis, we find the "four" and "twelve" to be as prominent as the "seven" in the case of Japheth. His name is 48,—4 times 12. His sons of the first grade are *four;* and three of these, with one of the second grade, making *four* in all, be-

---

* It might be called the city, or cosmical, number: the number of a well ordered State.

came fathers of nations; and, after deducting this one from the second grade, *four* remain; and Cush, the first-born, branches out into Nimrod, who founds *four* cities, and into Asshur, who also founds *four* cities. Thus the four is in every way the leading number. From *Mizraim*, however, there springs a *spiritual* number, for his descendants were *seven:* Egypt, in Scripture, always looks to the Church and has a mystic connection with it. From Canaan, on the contrary, comes the imperfect number eleven.

Shem has, in his name, the 300 of the church and the 40 of probation. His sons of the first class are *five*, the number of the law. From Arphaxad there are eight to Abraham, afterward developed to twelve in Jacob, but with a schismatical 13 in the days of Peleg, namely, Joktan's descendants.

Considering that earthly dominion began with Ham, legal religion with the race of Shem, while Japheth was reserved for the perfect day of the Spirit, these numbers are certainly appropriate.*

To return to the number seven and to our criterion: the result of all experiments is that seven enters into those dates of our A. M. column which are associated with its typical meaning, and *into no other dates* of that column whatsoever.†

If we try it by the equal list of figures in our second column, which figures (as explained before) are purely arbitrary, we find two dates only into which it divides.

---

* The whole number of names is 84, or 7 times 12.

† There are, however, two modern dates since added to the Table, into which it divides with very marked quotients, the Antichrist epochs of Bar Cochbas and Mohammed. These are considered in Chapter XV.

Thus seven, like eight, stands the twofold negative test.

In like manner the nine of Abraham is a factor of the following dates *only:* of the year of the Flood, the baptism by water; of the Exodus, when " our fathers were baptized unto Moses in the cloud and in the sea ;" of the baptism of our Lord, according to the estimate of Dr. Jarvis; and of that final baptism of fire and blood, the destruction of Jerusalem, which brought the church, the true ark of God, to the Ararat of this seventh age. These dates respectively are 1656, 2538, 4149, 4194 A. M. To these may be added the fiery baptism of Sodom, if we date that event from the year of Arphaxad.

In the second column it enters into six of the figures, *and into one of them appropriately.* For it happens to divide equally into 2016, the B. V. E. date of the destruction of Sodom and Gomorrah. Thus, out of all the figures to which the criterion has been applied, we have found, so far, only one instance of a coincidence that may be regarded as evidently casual. And even in this case there is something very remarkable. For if, in this instance, the A. M. date had followed the general rule and proved divisible by nine, the casual coincidence in the other column would have neutralized the force of the fact, so that one important epoch would have failed to contribute anything to the general appearance of design. As if to avoid this—as if it were intended to put the true coincidence in a position of marked contrast with the spurious one, the former is made to fall as it were from the regular ranks, and to reckon from Arphaxad instead of from Adam; from the beginning of its own special cycle rather than from that of the larger and more general cycle. On the whole, therefore, supposing the Divine object to be to *emphasize* certain ideas by connecting them numerically with certain marked events, the object is attained more fully by this anomaly in the date of Sodom, than if there had been no such anomaly. The baptism by fire is bound to the other baptisms* by *two* links instead of one.

The sum of it all is, in the case of Abraham, that his name may be compared to the scientific description of the "Topaz," which is "the ninth precious stone" in the "foundations of the wall" of the sacred city.† For it is said of this stone,‡ that its specific gravity is *three*, its hardness *eight*, "its hue *yellow* or *colorless*, but sometimes *green*, *blue*, or *red;*" and that "it crystallizes in the *trimetric* or rhombic system." So with the name Abraham: it has the "three" of the Trinity, the "eight" of the Resurrection, the "green" of the baptismal sea, the "blue" of the baptismal spirit,§ the

---

* Since writing the above, I have had occasion to add a few dates to the latter end of the Table, among which I find the time of *Herod* divisible by *Nine*—suggesting to the mind that *baptism of blood*, the martyrdom of the Innocents. For a fuller Table, including all the dates from Adam down to the decree of Artaxerxes, see Appendix B.

† Rev. xxi, 20.

‡ Appleton's "Cyclopædia," word *Topaz:* in quoting the numbers of this description, I omit the fractions.

§ The name *pneuma*, breath, air, spirit, is evidently a *symbolical* name of the Third Person of the Trinity: "the *breath* breatheth where it listeth . . . . so is every one that is born of the *breath*." So, in another place, our Lord *breathed* on the Disciples and said: "Receive ye the Holy Ghost." As the air, breathed almost unconsciously, sustains our natural life, so the Spirit sustains our spiritual life. In the case of the Israelites, this breath or air was condensed into "a cloud," and they were "baptized unto Moses "yellow" of the baptismal flame, the "red" of the baptismal blood, the "colorless" depth of the baptismal doctrine, while the whole "crystallizes in trimetric fashion," *three* times *three* by *three* times *three* times *three*—the thrice blessed, glorious, and adorable Triune God!

And this is brought out not by one or two odd coincidences, but at every turn and on every test. We find it in the name Abram; in the name Abraham; in his age, in his era; in the larger cycle of a complete six days of preparation. And not in one way only is the idea of the sacred Three and of baptism presented In the length of the ark, in its breadth, in its height, in its cubic contents, in the number of cubits that the flood prevailed, in the number of days that it endured, in its date; in the date of its nearest antitype, the fiery flood of Sodom; in that of the second antitype, the Red Sea flood; in that of the latest, the flood of desolation that overwhelmed Jerusalem; nay, in that of such secondary types as the baptism in blood of the Holy Innocents; and finally, in that which gives significance to all, the baptism of the Lord in the river Jordan. But even this does not exhaust the fulness of the coincidence. When we look to the measures of Solomon's Temple, and especially to those of the molten sea, we find there also a like prominence of the Abrahamic numbers. Can all this be chance? If so, it is at least a marvellous chance; a chance more wonderful, all things considered, than the other alternative, namely, that of a Divine intention.

in the Cloud and in the Sea." The sea they left behind: the Cloud remained with them—an image of the respective offices of the water and the Spirit.

Finally, let us apply our negative criterions to the number *thirteen*. In the first column it divides evenly into one date only, namely, the first year of Cyrus, the establishment of the Persian monarchy in Babylon and on the Euphrates. Considering the fact that Persia was for some centuries the most bitter of all countries in its persecution of Christianity, that afterward it was the seat of the great Nestorian schism, that finally it became the right arm of Mohammedanism, and that Babylon and the Euphrates are mystically associated in Scripture with the idea and the name of Antichrist, this coincidence is one that from our previous investigations we might have been led to expect. In the second column it divides into two dates, the call of Abraham and the *era of the Seleucidæ*. In this last instance, the coincidence is appropriate. For it marks the time when Seleucus took possession of Babylon and established a Greek dynasty there. Moreover, it was out of this dynasty or "head" of the Greek empire that Antiochus came, the first manifestation of "the little horn" of Daniel. Furthermore, as Forster* shows in his "Mohammedanism Unveiled," the Islamite manifestation of "the little horn" is intimately connected with the same head of the Grecian empire. Besides all which, the Seleucid Era, or Era of Contracts, is still recognized in the East. On the whole, therefore, *this* coincidence is certainly an appropriate one.

And *it may be*, in this instance, as in others before it, that the coincidence is not a mere matter of chance. For though the Vulgar Era is, in reference to Biblical chronology, an arbitrary one, so that in general no de-

* Vol. ii, p. 438 et ss.

pendence can be placed upon parallelisms that occur in connection with it, yet *in reference to modern history* it has a recognized place, and so long as Christianity endures it must continue to be an era universally accepted. Supposing, then, a supernatural *design* in the Scripture numerals, it is not impossible that this design, so far as modern history is concerned, may have a view in some cases to the *ordinary* Christian era, as well as to the more accurate epochs of the sacred chronology in general. It may be, in short, that where the sacred numbers link on to profane chronology, this link may be effected in two different ways. In the one case, it may be made with a view to *the true era*, the creation of the world: in the other, with a view to an arbitrary era, the assumed date of the Nativity.

And there is certainly one special feature of "the era of the Greeks," which might bring it fairly under a different rule from that which commonly applies. It not only began in post-Biblical times, but it is the epoch of a power *which came out of the nations*, and not, like Ishmael, out of the sacred family.

If this, however, should be deemed over subtle, and we should be forced to concede one or two coincidences to the freaks of chance, these one or two instances merely show *how often chance,* in such matters, *may be expected to tally with design.*

On the whole, taking our two columns of figures, tested in reference to four marked numerals, I have gone through about 320 experiments of division of dates by sacred factors. In the one column I have found some 16 cases of even division, every one of which is precisely what the principle in question requires: in the other, I have found some 24 cases, only two of which, and those doubtful ones, are found to accord with the principle.*

Stated mathematically, therefore, we have 318 successes to 320 experiments; for, of course, under the head of "successes," we count those which are elicited by the negative criterion, as well as those which depend on the positive. It is as remarkable, for instance, that eight should divide into *no other than* the Resurrection dates, as it is that it should divide into all of these.

On the other hand, our failures, supposing the two anomalous cases to come under that category, are only 2 to 320 experiments.

And even this does not cover the whole argument in favor of design. For in speaking of 320 experiments, I count only those which have been made on the Table of dates.† The equally curious results of our examina-

---

* I have since tried the experiment on a much larger scale, to the extent of about 100 dates in the A. M. column; and have found no *exception* to the rule which seems to govern the figures of that column, though in one or two instances the appropriateness of the factors is not so obvious as it has proved in the more prominent dates. See Appendix B. I find (among other things) that the year of the martyrdom of John Baptist divides by 7. As he is of the same type with Enoch and Elijah, this is quite striking.

† It has occurred to me to try these numbers by another test. The Scriptural dates, as given by Browne, differ from the table which I have used, in all the figures that follow the epoch of the covenant with Abraham. For Browne, in that place, *assumes* an epoch upon mere conjecture; whereas the one chosen by me is carefully dated in Scripture. This occasions a difference of 22 years in Abraham's epoch, and in all the dates that follow. It has occurred to me, therefore, to try Browne's dates by the numbers eight, seven, nine, and thirteen. The result is, that out of 27 dates,

tion of periods, or cycles, or incidental numbers, or the numerical significance of Hebrew names, I have left uncounted. I may add that these experiments are far more numerous than the others, those which I have given being but samples of a great mass which are equally striking and significant, though not so obviously connected with our chronological Table.

I cannot but repeat, that if all this is to be credited to the freaks of chance, chance is proved to be the most intelligent and most ingenious of wonder-workers.

in which we differ, two are divisible by 8, five by 7, three by 9, and one by 13, *without appropriateness or consistency* in any instance. I might say, therefore, 448 experiments instead of 320 have helped to prove the principle. I might also claim that the success of the experiments in the Table constructed on Abraham's covenant year, and the entire failure in that constructed on the other epoch, shows which of the two is in accordance with the *principle* of the sacred chronology.

CHAPTER XIV.

THE MEANINGS OF A FEW OTHER NUMERALS.

THERE are a few other numbers, more or less connected with the sacred chronology, the meanings of which have been *assumed* as a matter of convenience. I will now indicate a little more exactly some of the grounds of this assumption.

To expect that all of them should be capable of as rigid a proof as that which we have applied to the Numerals of the "Rest" and "Resurrection," would be unreasonable and against the analogy of Scripture. In matters of faith, there are always a few things strictly demonstrable. Other and secondary articles have to be received on the strength of these, or by reason of their harmony and agreement with them. Still, it will be found by any one who will take the pains to ascertain the mystic use of Scripture numerals, that they are almost as much within the range of accurate definition as are Scripture words, and that the process by which their meaning may be ascertained is not much more difficult. Indeed, it would be fully as easy, were it not for the neglect into which the whole subject has fallen in modern times.

The number *one* is, in all languages, a symbol, or rather a synonym of unity.

The number *three* I have assumed as a symbol of essential, the number *four* of organic, perfection.

As to *three*, it is well known that Scripture, like nature, like the human soul, and especially like the tri-literal Hebrew tongue, delights in this numeral: in its constant and significant recurrence throughout the sacred volume, and in its organic relation to the sacred language, "fanciful" persons, such as Origen, Augustine, Athanasius, and the saints and doctors generally of the olden time, have seen a certain foreshadowing of the doctrine of the Trinity. Modern Christians, of a more "logical" turn of mind, have set it all down to chance: though what "chance" is, and what is its precise office in God's word and work, "logic" has never been able to inform us. As a matter of "fact," however, apart both from "fancy" and "logic," there is a marked employment of this numeral in the sacred book. In the first chapters of Genesis,* there is "*God*" creating, there is "the *Spirit*" brooding upon the waters and quickening, there is "the *Lord* God," fashioning, contriving, ruling, and judging.

And in the second stage of history, Adam begets *one* son, Cain, who, though spiritually wicked, becomes a king of men,† founding cities, originating arts, taking the lead in one great object of human life, the subduing and replenishing of the earth. He begets a *second* son,

---

* Gen. i, ii, iii.

† The way in which the Scriptures do *justice* to the wicked, from Satan down, condemning their wickedness, but not concealing their grand qualities, or the grand part they play in human progress, is to my mind one of the peculiar marks of the Divinity of the Scriptures; in reference to Cain, let any one read and *ponder* Gen. iv.

Abel, who is a righteous seed, but withers before the breath of the wicked, and is cut off from among men. But in his *third* son, Seth, righteousness becomes a rooted and hardy growth. Or, if we count only by the spiritual succession: there is Adam *first*, Seth *second*, Enos *third;* and "*then* began men to call upon the name of the Lord."

And in the third stage of history, Noah, who is "the eighth" of the old world and "the first" of the new, begets *three* sons; and in those three again there are the three sides of perfection: in Ham, the beginning of dominion and of earthly civilization; in Shem, the preparatory day, the martyr period of religion; in Japheth, the ripe fruit of both, "the fruits of the Spirit." And when "the ark was a-preparing," it was so framed under the Divine direction as to embody in itself the chief of the sacred numbers. It was to be of *three* stories, with its height *three* tens, and its length *three* hundreds. Its breadth, however, was to be *five* tens, the number of Law; or perhaps fifty, the number of the jubilee. And of those that entered the ark, there were the *eight* of the Resurrection, the *sevens* of the Spirit, the *twos* of an imperfect or transitional stage. And of the times, there were the *six* centuries of Noah, and the *six* twenties of suspense, typical of the six great days of preparation for the kingdom; and the one *seven* of "rest," before the flood was upon the earth; and the *forty* of probation while "the rains descended;" and the "*fifteen* cubits," and the ten times *fifteen* days of the lifting up above the earth to the "second resurrection;" and again the "*seventh* month" of "rest;" and at last "the *first* year, *first* month, *first* day of the month," of a new existence, with the coming forth out of the ark by *one* and *three:* for "*Noah* went forth, and his *sons*, and his *wife*, and his *sons' wives* with him." Moreover, "Noah lived after the flood *three hundred and fifty years:*" the *three* hundred of the church and the *fifty* (it may be) of the jubilee.

"But all this is fancy." It may be so. Yet "fancy" is a true faculty of the human soul. It is one of God's good gifts.* No less than the much-vaunted "logical mind" has it the mark of the Divine image stamped upon it. Why should it be thought, then, "a thing impossible," that God should have furnished in His word some food for fancy, as well as the stronger meat which is craved by reason? Certainly His *works* are not all prose. Nor is the use of His works limited to prosaic and utilitarian ends. When we go out into the fields of a morning, and see every blade of grass arrayed in such diamonds as a queen might envy, of course we know that these are mere drops of water, "precipitated" during the night from an overcharged atmosphere, and that their *use* is to nourish and refresh the grass. But if they serve a purpose over and above this; if they enkindle the "fancy," and lift up the soul, and awaken thoughts of Him, "the dew of whose birth is of the womb of the morn-

---

* I cannot but think sometimes that if ever Astræa should come back to the earth, Fancy might justly bring in a suit against her sober partner, Reason. In matters of science, especially, the importance of Fancy is sadly underrated. Without her help there would be few discoveries in this world, few inventions. It so happens, however, that while it is really Fancy that makes all the useful and noble discoveries, Reason takes care to get out the patent for them, and so secures to herself the honor and profits.

ing," may we not reasonably argue that the dew drops were *intended* for something *more* than the nourishment of grass, or the solace of the cattle that feed upon it? But if we are allowed to reason thus with regard to God's works, who can blame us for so reasoning in reference to His word? The Bible, we all know, is not a "logical" book merely. It has the richness and redundancy of Oriental fancy. Nor is it a dry book, to be treated drily. It is all wet through and through with the dew of the Spirit. From a certain point of view and under a certain light its dew drops begin to flash and sparkle, as it were. There is a rainbow-like effulgence of celestial things. Nor is this a fickle, uncertain, inharmonious splendor. The same light flashes from Genesis to Revelation. Wherever or however we may see it, whether in types, or prophecies, or names, or numerals, or letters, everything seems to converge in that one bright vision, the vision seen by the holy seer in the isle of Patmos: when, "behold, a throne was set in heaven, and one sat on the throne. And he that sat was to look upon like a jasper and a sardine stone; and there was a rainbow round about the throne, in sight like unto an emerald: and round about the throne *four and twenty* seats; and upon the seats . . . four and twenty elders . . . clothed in white raiment; and out of the throne, . . . lightnings, and thunderings, and voices; and *seven* lamps of fire burning before the throne, which are the seven Spirits of God; and before the throne, a sea of glass like unto crystal; and in the midst of the throne *four* living creatures . . . each with *six* wings and full of eyes within: and they rest not day and night, saying, *Holy,*

holy, holy, Lord God Almighty, Which *was,* and *is,* and *is to come!*"

But this is a digression, which has diverted us from our inquiry into the use of the number *three.* Nor does it seem necessary to resume the inquiry. Any intelligent reader, who will take the pains to examine for himself, will find throughout the Old Testament and New, that not merely is this numeral one of constant recurrence, but that it enters into the whole organic structure of sacred history, and in a way so marked that, if we admit the idea of types at all, the significance of this type cannot possibly escape us. To trace out its use thoroughly would require a volume rather than the brief space I have here given to it. I will leave this numeral, therefore, with that "Holy, holy, holy," which it everywhere suggests, and will say a few words about the number *four.*

It is found in the *name* of Adam, whose letters are the *one* of unity, the *forty* of probation, the *four* of dominion or organization; while the sum of his name is *nine* times *five.*

It is found in *Eden,* where it stands, as in Adam, midway between two other significant numerals, namely, the *seventy* and *seven hundred** of peace or rest. And the river of Eden divides into "*four* heads," the first of which (not perhaps without a meaning) compassed a land of "gold," and of "bdellium and the onyx stone:" from Adam's day to the present, "gold" and "dominion" are closely associated. It is found in Cain, whose name, according to one rendering, would be 160, the *forty* of probation multiplied by *four,* or, according to another, 810, which is three to the *fourth*

---

* Or, according to the lesser value, the 50 of Jubilee: the whole being 124, four times the number of Deity.

power multiplied by ten, a symbol of the heavenly perverted to earthly ends. It is a factor of the name of Cainan, the *fourth* from Adam, which is 860, or four times two hundred and fifteen. It comes out most prominently, as mentioned in the preceding chapter, in the name and genealogy of Ham, who, in respect of earthly power and civilization, as also of irreverence, is the Cain of the world after the flood. Among the sons of Jacob, Judah was the *fourth;* and to him fell the dominion over all his brethren.

In nature, there are the *four* quarters of the world, the *four* feet of the highest order of beasts, the *four* elements; besides which it is the first *square* among numerals, and has other associations too numerous to mention.

Its use in Scripture makes it the symbol of heavenly as well as of earthly order. There are not only the " four beasts" coming up out of the sea, and the " four heads" of empire, but also the " four-square city," and the " four living creatures " which have their place in that city.

In the same way, as has been noticed before, *twelve*, the marked multiple of four and three, has an earthly as well as a sacred application.

In short, *four* is the cosmical number, the number of creation, organization, dominion, the number of organic as distinguished from essential perfection. Its scriptural use in this sense might be largely illustrated, if necessary.

The number *two* is the symbol of a transitional or intermediate stage. It is a number of insufficiency or expectancy: which meaning appears more strongly in its multiples *twenty* and *two hundred*.

The Incarnation, which is a seeming exception to this meaning, being the union of *two* natures in one person, is really a proof of the rule. For the Incarnation, to do its perfect work, required that He, the incarnate Word, should go unto the Father and send " another Comforter : " so that there again the *two* points the way and leads to three. Even Christ we are not " to know after the flesh ; " " it is the Spirit that quickeneth." So, also, in the " mystery " of holy wedlock, " they *twain* shall be one flesh : " yet not in themselves, but " in the Lord."

Six, for a different reason, is a number of earthly imperfection. It is the *six* of the work-day world, not yet crowned by the *seven* of rest in the Spirit. Its concentrated force is found in the 666 of " the beast," that is, of the earthly *opposed* to the spiritual power. But the earthly is not necessarily antagonistic to the spiritual : it is *in need* of the Spirit ; it is defective and imperfect, not positively evil. Hence 6, 60, and 600 are generally indicative of this milder sense.

The six days or periods of the imperfect, preparatory world, have frequently been alluded to in the course of this Inquiry. There were " six steps " to the throne of Solomon, the peaceful prince. So by " six steps " the world ascended to the pacific reign of Christ. The same thought was beautifully drawn by the Fathers from the " six water-pots " of our Lord's first miracle in Cana. For the " water," they would say, is typical of the peoples ; the vessels containing the water are emblems of the ages ; the conversion of the water into wine is that great miracle by which " He manifested forth His glory," namely, the infusion into the ages of a higher life, the conversion of the world into a fitness for the bridal feast of the Lamb. His first miracle, therefore, was a "sign" of the great spiritual miracle. It was an earnest of the work the Gospel was destined to accomplish. There seems to be something of the same allusion in "the chambers against the wall" of Solomon's Temple.* For the nethermost chamber was *five* cubits broad, and the middle was *six* cubits broad, and the third was *seven* cubits broad. The *six*, based upon the Law and perfected by the Spirit, is an epitome of the history of the human race. In Ezekiel's vision,† also, the Temple is measured by a "reed *six* cubits long;" and the porch, the gate, the threshold, and all the "little chambers" of preparation, are just "*six* cubits." Other numbers come as we advance farther in. The door-way, especially, is "*six* cubits," but the breadth of the door itself is "*seven* cubits."

I may notice, also, in reference to our Table of sacred dates, that the two great *finial* epochs, the end of the world before the flood, and the end of the Levitical dispensation, are both divisible by six, with figures in the quotients which are capable of appropriate meanings. Taken in connection with the results of previous inquiries, this fact is worth remarking.‡

Five, among the Hebrews, was the unit of military organization. Thus, "Israel went up harnessed," or, as otherwise translated, "*five in a rank*, out of the land of Egypt." So with many other places. The proverbial phrase, "*five* of you shall chase an hundred," derived much of its force from this fact. The number is more commonly associated with the Pentateuch, or five books of Moses, and is used as a symbol of the Law. Its frequent recurrence in connection with the Tabernacle is very striking: "*five* curtains," "*five* bars,"

---
* Kings vi. 6. † Ezek. xl, xli. ‡ See Appendix C.

"*five* pillars," "*five* sockets," the altar "*five* cubits long, *five* cubits broad," the "height of the hangings *five* cubits." So, in the New Testament, it is often used *as if* with a mystic reference. There are the "*five* porches" of Bethesda; the "*five* barley loaves" which fed the "*five* thousand;" the "*four* thousand," however, a phrase suggestive of the city of God, were fed with "*seven* loaves."

Nine I have assumed as a symbol of paternity, chiefly from its prominence in the name of Adam, the father of mankind, and of Abram, "the father of highness." There are other facts looking in the same direction. If this be a true conjecture, it adds another to the reasons already given for regarding *thirty-one* as the number of Deity. For *nine* being the symbol of the Father, *eight* of the Son, *seven* of the Spirit; and the Spirit proceeding from the Father *and* the Son: we should have 9 and 7 *plus* 7 and 8 as the full arithmetical expression of the doctrine of the Trinity.

Ten is naturally associated with the commandments. As a factor or multiplier it gives an intensive force to other numerals.

I have thus indicated the mere starting-points of such associations of ideas as might serve to fix the meaning of some of the principal numerals. I do not pretend to have given the best definitions. To do justice to the subject in its wider range, it would be necessary to make a thorough analysis of the numbers connected with the Ark, the Tabernacle, the Temple, the vision of Ezekiel, the book of Revelation, and perhaps of Exodus, Numbers, and other historical books. It would also be necessary to go much farther than I have ventured into the whole subject of scriptural symbolism. I have thought it best to confine myself to the numerals of chronology. Those which I have noticed,* and perhaps a few others not noticed here, are all more or less connected with that fruitful subject.

* The line of thought which has been indicated in this chapter, perhaps too slightly to do justice to it, is the *extreme* application of a *principle*, upon the reception or rejection of which our belief in Inspiration must ultimately depend. We take, for example, the distinction, that so much has been made of, between the Jehovistic and Elohistic portions of Genesis. Either this distinction is, as the Fathers believed it to be, the result of a Divine intention, *having a deep significance wherever it occurs*, or else it was a mere careless following of one or other of several ancient documents. The latter theory is inconsistent with any real belief in Divine Inspiration. For even a human writer, if he really knows what he is about, would never use such words at random. If he says "Lord" instead of "God," or the reverse, it is because he wishes to convey some shade of meaning by the word he uses, which would not be conveyed by the other word. None but an empty and shallow declaimer will deliberately *write* words, without a special meaning. When it is conceded, therefore, that Moses used the one word or the other, in a matter of such grave importance as the name of Deity, merely because the one or the other happened to be before him in some supposed ancient document, we put Moses below the level of all really good writers. The early Church would never have admitted such an idea. They believed in Scripture as a living organism. Nothing was without an intention; nothing without a meaning. At the present day, we are too much disposed to abandon this high ground, chiefly (I think) because we have abandoned the *minute* study of the Scriptures. Were we to deal with the sacred Word as men of science have learned to deal with the facts of nature, we might find reason to return to the higher ground, and to contend for every word, every syllable, every grammatical inflexion, as having a propriety of its own. This, of course, may be carried too far. But how far it may be carried is a legitimate subject of inquiry, and even of experiment. Especially is it a subject of " free inquiry "—which, I would again remind the reader, is the object of this book.

CHAPTER XV.

THE MYSTIC NUMBERS A KEY TO CHRONOLOGY.

We have seen, from a close examination of the numbers eight, seven, nine, thirteen, that those figures at least have a definite significance in Scripture, over and above their arithmetical value.

It has furthermore appeared that this inner or mystic meaning is not a happy coincidence merely, a thing to be explained by the doctrine of chances, but that it is inwoven into the whole texture of Scripture language, and has to an extraordinary degree the marks of an elaborate system.

Having proved this in the case of these leading figures, and having indicated the grounds that exist for ascribing certain meanings to the less important numerals, I will now call attention, as briefly as possible, to the additional light shed upon our Table by the results of our inquiry, and to the conclusive evidence thus afforded of its thoroughly systematic and consistent character.

And *first*, as to those periods of time which we have designated as Jerusalem, Israel-Judah, or Abrahamic terms. In giving them these titles originally, I was little aware of the propriety of the names thus chosen.

The term of 450 years, for example, I called "Abrahamic," chiefly because it introduced the great crisis of the life of Abraham. So also with the 490 years: the name "Jerusalem term" was selected because the period was spoken of by Daniel as "determined upon . . . *the holy city.*"

But now we are in a position to see a deeper propriety, both in the names and numbers. Jerusalem, for example, is the type of the New Jerusalem, the Heavenly City, the "dwelling of peace" or "rest," the kingdom or polity of this "seventh" day. Accordingly, its number is *seventy sevens.* And this term of "seventy sevens" of years is, as we have seen, *four* times repeated. Why "four times"? Because "four" is emphatically the city number. The heavenly city is built "four-square." Eden, its first type, is in its numerals 70 and 4 and 700; and in its description the most prominent feature is the river that "was parted, and became into *four* heads." Had it been our object to invent a numerical symbol expressive of the idea of the sacred city, could we have framed one more beautiful and significant than this "seventy sevens" multiplied by "four"?

Again, 430 is the "Israel-Judah term." Its elements are 40 for Judah, the Resurrection number multiplied by the number of the Law; and 390 for Israel, the schism number multiplied by the same, and again multiplied by "six," the number of earthly imperfection. And the whole combined is 86 multiplied by 5; which 86, again, is 80, a multiple of the Resurrection number, with the addition of 6, the number of imperfection. Finally, this "Israel-Judah term" is *five* times repeated. It belongs to the legal dispensation.

The "number" of that dispensation *determines* the number of times the period is made to recur.

Once more, 450 is the "Abrahamic term." The connection of this number with the name of Abram has been sufficiently shown in a preceding chapter. But why are there *six* Abrahamic terms? The answer is obvious. The Abrahamic cycle is larger than that of "the law." It embraces the whole idea of "preparation" for Christ: it symbolizes the entire six days of the "imperfect" world, of the world waiting for its Lord, waiting for its sacred "rest." Nothing could be more proper, then, than that there should be six Abrahamic days.

Thus, there are *four* "Jerusalem terms," *five* "Israel-Judah terms," *six* "Abrahamic terms." The symmetry of this result strikes me more forcibly now, because at first I was a little disappointed by it. Not being aware of the type relation of the "four," the "five," and the "six," I was disposed to look for the symmetry in another form, and to search for *six* "terms" for all the three names alike.

As it is, there is not uniformity, but harmony and consistency; a thing more beautiful in itself, and a surer mark of design.

So again: looking back at our list of symmetrical periods, one would naturally ask, Why are there *twelve* of the Judah terms? Because "twelve" is the national number, and Judah, as we know, was the centre of national unity. And why do the Israel or Ephraim terms go always by *sixes?* "Six," as mentioned before, is the number of "preparation" in the larger or vaguer sense. Israel, though schismatic and apostate, had its share in the grand work of preparing the way for the Lord; only it had not the definite and organic share which fell to the lot of Judah. Hence the Israel number, as we have noticed, is a measure, not only of the Ephraim schism, but of the whole Abrahamic or Arphaxad cycle. Again: Why do the *seventies* and the *thousands* so overlap one another as to make a kind of image of *three*-in-*one?* The seventies and the thousands are figures of the reign of Christ. Keeping this in view, no one need be reminded why the Three-in-One should come out so clearly in that connection. Again: Why do the *twenties* appear *nine* times? Nine is the number of Abraham; and Abraham, as mentioned before, is a type of patient expectancy. Again: Why is *forty* the Judah term, and *three hundred and ninety* the term of Ephraim? As already mentioned, the answer is found in the spiritual meanings of the factors eight, five, thirteen, six, and the like. Yet once more: Why are the *seventy weeks* of Daniel introduced by a seven,* and emphasized by prominent epochs in just seven places? The propriety of the number is obvious on a moment's reflection.

Furthermore, the classification by *threes*, above alluded to, extends much farther than is there indicated, and with great significance in all cases. Not only the *seventies* and *thousands* make a kind of three-in-one, but there is something of the same arrangement of the *four hundred and eighties*. Two of these periods have been pointed out: namely, the 480 of 1 Kings vi, 1, preparatory to Solomon's Temple, and the mystic twelve forties preparatory to the true and living

---

* Besides the 70 and 70 and 70 and 7, introducing the "seventy weeks," the actual number of years included by those overlapping seventies is 147: or $7 \times 7 \times 3$.

Temple. There is a third, typical of these, between Noah's birth and the 120 years of "suspended judgment," *preparatory to the building of the Ark*. Thus, as the Ark was in three stories and the Temple in three parts, and the living Temple in the name of the sacred Three, so there were three of the mystic 480 years of preparation. So, again, the *twelve* forties, which make up the 480, go by threes: three of provocation, three of humiliation or defeat, three of deliverance, three of extended empire. In short, each kind of "probation" is perfected in the sacred Three. The prevalence of this number in the Ark has been shown in a previous chapter. It has an equal prominence in Solomon's Temple. Besides the three parts, there are three "chambers round about;" and the "molten sea," containing 3,000 baths, is compassed by a line of 30 cubits, on which are 300 knops; and of the 12 oxen which supported it, "there were three looking toward the north, and three looking toward the west, and three looking toward the south, and three looking toward the east." And this is the precise order,* by the way, in which the gospel of the sacred Three went out from Jerusalem: first "toward the north," Samaria, Damascus, Antioch; next "toward the west," Cæsarea, Cyprus, Corinth, Rome; next "toward the south," Alexandria and Egypt; finally "toward the east," Mesopotamia, Persia, India. So, in many other ways, the number three is connected with the Temple as intimately as with the Ark.

* There is no other connection in Scripture, in which the four quarters of the world are mentioned in this order: a fact that gives additional significance to the type. Moreover, in *this* connection, both Kings and Chronicles give the *same* order.

To return to the chronology: the mystic term 40 *and* 65 also recurs three times. It first comes out in connection with Seth, who lived "one hundred and five years," which is 40 and 65, "and begat Enos:" and "*then men began to call on the name of the Lord.*" In the two other instances, its appearance is the forerunner of a similar result. It preceded the Captivity, in which Israel and Judah were purged of idolatry, so that afterward they bore everywhere a steadfast witness to the unity of the Godhead : it preceded the final dispersion, which was the era of a *new* calling on the name of the Lord, the name of the sacred Three. There are also three *four hundred and thirties*, "determined" by important epochs.* The first is from the Covenant to the Exodus; the second, from the end of Joshua and the Elders to David; the third, from the Dedication of the Temple to the Captivity. Thus, the larger Israel-Judah term leads to the same end as the shorter. Both are perfected by a trine repetition. Both lead to a captivity, a dispersion, a destruction of the Temple made with hands: a "captivity," however, which was really to give liberty; a "dispersion," which was preparatory to a more complete gathering; a destruction, from which a new Temple was to emerge, the true and living House of God.

There are other examples of the trine arrangement. But to pass them by, and to bring those that have been mentioned under one point of view, we find that the idea of "rest," as seen in the seventies; of "probation" in its four forms, as typified in the forties; of "prepa-

---

* The same applies to the 450's: the Arphaxad Patriarchs, the Judges, the Kings—each series 450 years, making altogether $3 \times 3 \times 3$ jubilees.

ration" for the Ark or Temple, as in the four hundred and eighties; of the "calling and election," as in the Israel-Judah terms; of "glory and dominion," as in the millenniums: all are intimately associated with the sacred Three, and the frequency of their recurrence in a marked or "determined" way seems to be regulated by that significant number.

So much for the general "harmony and consistency" of the mystic numbers and the chronology.

But there is not only a "harmony and consistency," there is also a nice gradation in the several terms. The "Abrahamic" cycle, the most comprehensive, dates from the birth of Shem; the "Israel-Judah," from the Covenant with Abraham; the "Jerusalem," from the Exodus. The scope of "election" narrows by degrees. There is first the wider range of patriarchal faith; then the special "call" and the "covenant;" lastly, the well-defined worship of the "four-square city." Yet again, each of these terms goes back, as it were, behind itself, so as to take hold upon the term preceding. The Abrahamic cycle begins in the old world before the flood; that of Israel-Judah reaches back to Abraham. That of Jerusalem commences long before Jerusalem was the sacred city. The earlier dispensation foreshadows the later: the later takes the earlier into itself. This is beautifully shown in that largest Israel-Judah cycle, the *sixty-five* times *forty*, or 2,600 years, which begins with Arphaxad and rolls on to the final dispersion. In short, there is not merely a symmetry and gradation in the various terms, but an elaborate interlacing: each bound to each, like the successive stages of life, by "natural piety."

And in connection with this we may note a very

curious and very significant fact, with regard to the millennial period, the "thousand years" of the Book of Revelation.

There was a well-known tradition among the Jews, as well as among the Christians of the early Church, that the Messiah was to come at the end of the sixth millennium, and that his reign was to endure just one thousand years. The notion is alluded to in the Epistle of Barnabas:* "As God finished His works in six days, so in six thousand years the Lord is bringing † things to a close .... for one day is with the Lord as a thousand years." In accordance with which St. Barnabas speaks of "*the eighth* day" as "the beginning of the other world." This tradition the Jews, according to their wont, interpreted in a literal and fleshly way. They expected Christ to come precisely at the end of six thousand years; and as the Hebrew chronology extended at that time to only four thousand years, the earlier coming of the Messiah furnished them with an argument against the Gospel.

Our Table shows that they were right in their notion of six great days of preparation. Those days, divided from each other by solemn judgments, are so manifest that one can hardly miss them. But the whole scheme of the chronology shows that the economy of "the times and seasons" was not based upon the large round numbers, but upon a much more elaborate and suggestive plan. Thus the average day, as we have shown, proves not to be "one thousand years," but 699 years, a day of Noah *plus* a day of Abram, a preparation for

---

* Barnab. *Epistol.* xv.

† I translate by the *present* tense, instead of the future, because (it seems to me) the context requires it.

the baptism by water *plus* a preparation for the baptism by fire. The word "thousand," in fact, is so often used vaguely in Scripture, that, to express a "set time," or determined period, it would be less suitable on the whole than most other numbers. While the Jews were right, therefore, in looking for six days, or even for six millenniums, they erred in giving to those millenniums a carnal interpretation.

Yet it is remarkable that *one* of those days of preparation *was* a millennium precisely. From the Exodus to the destruction of Solomon's Temple, that is, the fifth day of our series, *the day of the Law, and Theocracy, and Temple, and of the unbroken possession of Canaan*, there were exactly a thousand years: and, as if to *emphasize* this, there is another millennium, overlapping the one just mentioned, and almost as precisely marked, which extends from the Temple to the Nativity; or, this last date being uncertain, from the end of Solomon's reign to the year of John the Baptist.

The number one thousand, then, is intimately connected with the day of Jerusalem. It occurs then, and then only, in the chronological series, when the Temple and City of God, the celestial polity, were most unequivocally foreshadowed.

As to the bearing of all this upon the millennium typified by it,* the "thousand years" of "the first resurrection," I would not venture to express any decided opinion. This much may be noticed, however, without pretending in any way to lift the prophetic veil, that as the millennium of the Theocracy was able (as it were) to *reproduce* itself; as it contained within itself the germ of another millennium which shot out from the

* Rev. xx, 4, 5.

first and extended unto the Advent; so it may prove with the millennium of the Book of Revelation. It may be *a measure* of the reign of Christ, of the duration of His Kingdom here on earth, but not a rigid expression of its exact length in years. Moreover, *how* that measure is to be applied, how the "thousand years" of prophecy are to be adjusted to the years of history, may be precisely that one element which God, in His wisdom, has not seen fit to reveal. Prophecy, at most, points to the door of the future. The key to that door is in the hands of the event.

But this *germinating* power which I have spoken of in connection with the millenniums, appears so often in the "times and seasons," that it may be reckoned among the *principles* of sacred chronology. It is the power by which a period propagates itself after its own kind, just as one joint of a reed contains in itself another, which in due time it puts forth. This is shown in the three "seventies" that precede the "seventy sevens." In the same way the "seventy sevens," as they draw to a close, show a similar disposition, and the last "half-week" of that famous period projects itself, as it were, into the "three years and a half" of the Antichrist Bar Cochbas. But connected with this last there is another phenomenon more curious still. The year 132, when this great enemy of Christ seized on Jerusalem, is 4256 A. M., a figure divisible both by *seven* and *eight*. The presence of these two numerals led me, when I first observed it, to expect something remarkable, and perhaps prophetic, in relation to the Antichristian power. Could it be for a while a "rest," as the number *seven* would indicate, and then (according to *eight*) a *revival* or "resurrection" of that power?

I looked at the date of the Hegira, 622, the great day of Mohammedanism,* and found it to be precisely 490 years from the year above mentioned. The "seventy sevens," then, are not by any means exhausted when they come to the Christian era. It is a living and pregnant term. It goes on, and perhaps will go on, "even until *the* consummation." For, as the prophecy of Daniel was fulfilled, yet with a germ of other fulfilments, in the "week" of our Lord's ministry, so it may be with the number "determined upon" it. The "people," the "city," the fateful "number," are all still alive. What their future may be the event alone can show.

But to go back to the millenniums: as the one which synchronizes with the fifth day of our Table is found to germinate, and put forth another after it, so *it* also in like manner came out from a preceding one, namely, from that which measures the interval between Abraham and Solomon. Thus, the 40 of the son of David, the reign of "peace" and the time of building the Lord's House, is the living germ of the millenniums. One leads to it, another embraces it, a third comes out from it. And this third one leads to Christ, the true Prince of Peace.

And in connection with this "fifth day," I am reminded that, while the octave or "eight" is the most perfect harmony, "five" comes next to it in the harmonic scale. This being the case, the prominence of the fifth day or period, and the tone it gives to the entire seven days, is not the least remarkable among

---

* The Hegira date, 4746, divides by *Seven times Six*, that is by *forty-two*, yielding as a quotient one hundred and *thirteen*. Taken in connection with the name and number of Ishmael, this is very curious and consistent.

the coincidences revealed in our Table. The Law, the theocracy, the promised land, the Temple, the Prince of Peace, the fountain-head of the millenniums, all are contained in this marked numeral. And in profane history we notice phenomena of a parallel kind. This was emphatically the epoch of *history*. The "waters" brought forth "abundantly the moving creature that hath life, and fowl to fly above the earth in the open firmament of heaven." The four "great beasts" which came "up out of the sea," all have their beginning in "this fifth day." The "lion" of Assyria had learned to "stand on its feet as a man," and ("a man's heart being given" to it) was advancing in humane and liberal culture. The Medo-Persian "bear" was beginning to turn on its side. The "leopard" of Greek wisdom was developing its grace and painted skin and aromatic fragrance. The she-wolf of the West was suckling her human whelps, and Numa and Egeria were drawing from the fountain of Grecian wisdom the elements of a milder and more elevated nurture. In short, the "dominant" of the harmony had been struck in this fifth era.* One note more, the sixth, carries on the ascending scale. Then comes a seventh, a peculiar tone, a discord, a "rest;" till finally the grand octave opens, and the harmony of God's days is perfect in the eight of the resurrection.

It is part of the plan of this inquiry not to shrink

---

* The *Third* is next to the Fifth in perfection: and it was the third Day of Creation, in which *life* began. The Fifth was the epoch of *higher* life. The Eighth is that day for which "the earnest expectation of the creature waiteth." In history, also, the third Day, or period, was the *seed-time* of the nations, the manifestation of life in its lower types.

from the minuter applications of principles that come before us, even though in some cases the minuteness is such as may seem to border on the frivolous. In the word of God, as in His work, the little things are often the decisive things. The world revealed to us by the microscope is not less wonderful, or less divine, than the larger field opened by the telescope.

I will therefore refer to *the name* Jerusalem in connection with this period of "one thousand years." Jerusalem, "the Vision of Peace," or, according to Gesenius, "the Home or Dwelling of Peace," is 216 for that part of the word translated "dwelling," and three hundred and seventy for *Salem*, "peace." The meaning of these last figures has frequently been alluded to. The number 216 is *three* to the third power, a concentrated form of the sacred triad, multiplied by eight, the resurrection number. Analogous to this is the number of the millennium. It is five to the third power, multiplied by the eight of the resurrection. In the *extreme* analysis, then, in the minutest fibres as it were of "the day of Jerusalem," in the very dust of the golden streets of that "four-square" city, there is still the same vivid pulse of "thoughts that breathe." The Trinity, the resurrection, the rest and peace, the church which is founded upon the sacred Three, with the four of organization and the five of Law, the Law not abolished, but fulfilled in Christ: all come before us at every turn; all are repeated with endless variations, but in proportions beautiful, symmetrical, and full of spiritual meaning.

The numbers of Solomon's Temple have also a bearing in this direction; but, to do justice to them, one would have to go into the subject of mystical numbers in general. I will therefore confine myself to one fact. The oracle of the Temple was, like the celestial city, "four-square;" "the length and the breadth and the height of it (were) equal." Its cubic contents were *twenty* to the third power, or 8,000 cubits; which is the "thousand" of the millennium multiplied by the "eight" of the resurrection.

Thus, whichever way we turn, whether to dates, periods, names, or architectural details, whether to the sober facts of history or to the bright visions of seers and prophets, we find the numerals of Scripture to be organically bound together. Chronology, as a general rule, is the driest of all studies. No subject is less likely to excite the imagination. But with Biblical chronology it is an entirely different thing. Its dates and terms are full of spirit and of life. We sit down to it, perhaps, as to a sum in arithmetic. But before we are aware, we are carried we know not whither. Eden is before us with its river of four heads; the Ark, with its mystic freight; Sodom, with its fiery baptism; Jerusalem, with its gates of pearls and its walls of precious stones, are conjured up before us by the spell of a few ciphers; and while we are still lingering on the threshold of chronology, we find ourselves involved in the deepest questions of divine truth.

And the secret of all this, I think, is that the Bible is "a living thing." It is a thing that we can hardly touch without touching a nerve. And who can touch a nerve, without a thrill through his whole frame that proclaims what it is he touches?

I will not detain the reader with further examples of those symmetries which are the subject of this chapter. The Table is full of them; and to many of them, and to their connection with the numbers seven, eight, nine, thirteen, and the like, attention has been directed in the course of our investigation.

It may not be amiss to add that this Table was drawn up and *finished* before the symmetries spoken of in this chapter had come before my mind. The inquiry into the force of mystic numbers has revealed many features of it which otherwise might have passed unnoticed; but it has not caused me to alter a single figure in it. The line of study by which it was constructed, and that by which it has been illustrated, are entirely distinct.

Note. In connection with the 12 Forties, in this Chapter, and in Chapter X, I may also mention that there are 12 Forties of *days*, as well as of years: namely, seven which are described as "forty days and forty nights," and five, simply as " 40 days." Of these three are with God "in the Mount," namely, Moses twice and Elijah once; three are in vicarious humiliation, Moses twice and Ezekiel once; and the remaining six are not so easy to classify. Besides the 12 *historical* forty years, there is one prophetical, three times mentioned, pertaining to Egypt—Ezek. xxix, 11-13; and there are eight relating to the lives of individuals—e. g., Joshua was " forty years old," when Moses sent him to spy out the land.

CHAPTER XVI.

THE SCHEME SUPERNATURAL.

We have brought out the marks of design in the numerals of Scripture. I come now to the question, What is the nature of this design? Is it natural or supernatural? Can it be attributed to the ingenuity of man, or has it the sure marks of a plenary inspiration?

1. I see a proof of its divine character, *first*, in the entire *simplicity* of the principle that underlies it.

This principle, as I have more than once said, is that of *a simple, child-like-association of ideas*. This is its beauty from one point of view, its reproach from another. But no thinking man need be told that, whether it be a beauty or a reproach, it is at all events in accordance with God's ways, as seen in the laws of nature. It is the very simplicity of those laws that makes them so difficult to find out. More than five thousand years men had seen apples fall, without its once occurring to them that there was anything in that spectacle more than the fall of an apple. But at length the phenomenon came under the eyes of a great child-soul. And what was the result? The apple germinated, and grew into a type of the universe.

And if there be anything more than an accident in

the subject of mystic numbers, it will be found that all knowledge of the subject must start from premises equally obvious and simple. A "casual" word in one place causes the mind to glance off to the same word in another. Then a third place occurs. Among all these places there seems to be a certain living connection. Is it chance, or is it design? We begin to investigate. And so we are led on by steps so easy and natural, that we feel almost ashamed of the simplicity of the thing, and are tempted to pass it by as unworthy of the Divine greatness.

But God is great in small things. His is a simple greatness. He can put more into a mustard-seed than man could pack up in a whole world. When I find, therefore, that the principle which we have examined is such as a child can comprehend, but which a man would be apt to stumble at, it is an evidence to my mind that the system which grows out from it is not human, but Divine.

2. Another proof of its divine character lies in the seeming opposite of this: namely, in the minuteness and intricacy of its subtle ramifications.

I can imagine the possibility that *one* man, supposing him to be a genius of the highest order, a poet, a philosopher, an able mathematician, might so compose a book, that a subtle vein of sublime thought should underlie its letter, and be intelligible to those only who should have the key to its interpretation. But to do it with such skill that the very numerals employed, the very letters of sacred names, should be made to crystallize, as it were, around certain ideas and dates far back in the past or forward in the future; and that each number and name and date should refuse so to crystallize around any but its own idea: this, it seems to me, is beyond the reach of human genius.

And even if it were possible for one man, would it be possible for other men, in a long series extending over more than a thousand years, to take up so subtle a system, and to carry it out consistently, and to preserve its exact proportions, and to present it finally in such symmetry as that which we have seen?

Now this, in truth, is the marvel of the Scriptures, both in great things and small. The harmony of the Divine word is the proof of its inspiration. And when this harmony appears in such intricacies and minutiæ as those we have examined; when a certain *play* upon words and ciphers, occurring in one place, is seen to dimple (as it were) the whole face of Scripture, so that from Genesis to Revelation the great deep smiles;[*] nay, when this extends to so dry a subject as matter-of-fact chronology; when the tally of time's calendar, all notched and scored with the marks of thousands of years, suddenly, like Aaron's rod, breaks out into buds and blossoms: then it becomes next to impossible not to see the finger of God in it, and to attribute it to man appears the height of philosophic credulity.

But it may perhaps be argued that the system, as we have sketched it, proves too much. If the number eight, for example, divides equally into dates connected with the idea of the Resurrection, *and into none other*, where is the limit to all this? If the names of type-characters in Scripture can be resolved into numbers corresponding to the type idea, how far does this apply

---

[*] ────── ποντίων τε κυμάτων
ἀνήριθμον γέλασμα.
Prometh. Vinct. 89.

to other Scriptural names? Is there no end to this subtle play upon words, and names, and figures?

Of course there is a limit. With regard to dates, for instance, every year is a date for one event or another; and, if Scripture chronology were made out for each consecutive year, doubtless many multiples of eight would occur, without the slightest reference to the idea of the Resurrection.* It is enough to prove design, if a table of prominent dates only, of such dates as would be selected on natural grounds of preference, is found to involve the rule or principle we have noticed.

And so with all the other symmetries, coincidences, or types. The limit of their occurrence would be found to be in conformity with the Divine *purpose* in their occurrence. Because miracles are wrought sometimes, it does not follow that they must always be wrought. And what is true of the greater miracles is true of the lesser. These symmetries, for example, *may* have been intended as a kind of *evidence of the supernatural* in Scripture. If so, the symmetries would extend as far as they might be needed in the way of evidence, and probably no farther. Or they may have been intended as a kind of *stimulus* to the minute study of God's word. If so, they would hardly occur oftener than would conduce to that end. And there can be no question that they served that purpose in the early Christian church. No men have ever studied the Bible as the Fathers did in the times of the first six centuries. For they studied it not as critics, but as lovers. And one thing, unquestionably, that gave zest to their study of

* See Appendix B.

it was their keen appreciation of the beauty of its symbols.

Again, these symmetries of Scripture, occurring as they do in connection with so matter-of-fact a thing as the arithmetic of chronology, may have been intended as a corrective to an excessive and grovelling fondness for *mere* matter of fact. There is no doubt, of course, that this is a work-day world, and that man as a general rule is put here to work. But does he work any the worse for an occasional glimpse of the blue sky? Does the prose of human life necessarily exclude its poetry? That the Bible, on the whole, takes the sunny side of life; that it sings rather than preaches; that it marries poetry to prose, and cries Woe! to him who would sunder that blessed tie; that from Genesis to Revelation it is a grand choral *Sursum Corda*, is obvious to every one who really loves the Bible. And this poetic character may be stamped upon it for a purpose. And if it is found to enter even into its minutiæ, if even its arithmetic ciphers hymns rather than sums, this might still be useful as a reminder that Heaven is nearer to us than we think: it might teach us that in all things there is an element of the divine, if only we would look up and see it.

In short, we can imagine many purposes that might be answered by such a system as that which has been sketched. Yet, whatever the purpose might be, the system of course would be limited by a due subordination to that purpose.

It is no argument, then, against the fact of a mystical use of numbers, to say that such a use in one case would imply a similar use in all. The question is simply one of fact. In some cases, and under some circumstances, there is such a use. To ascertain in what cases, and under what circumstances, and with what limitations, would require much care and study; more, perhaps, than could be brought to bear upon it by any one mind.

3. I see a proof of the supernatural in *the latency* of the chronological system of the Bible.

The system which we have traced depends upon *two or three links* in the long chain of dates; and those links would have been lost beyond all recovery, except for *two* seemingly *casual utterances* of St. Paul, and *one* utterance of like character from St. Stephen, the first martyr.

It depends also, and almost equally, upon two dates, that of the fall of Jerusalem under Titus, and that of the final catastrophe under Hadrian, which lie outside of the Scriptures, in ordinary history.

Without these three utterances and these two dates, the chronology of the Bible, with all its carefully recorded items, would appear purposeless and nerveless; a broken spine, as it were; a telegraphic cable laid at prodigious cost under the deep sea, but sundered at some point where no skill can mend it.

But apply to the broken chronology these "casual" utterances: at once it starts out in symmetrical proportions. Apply to it further these two dates of common history: at once it lives and breathes, a "thing of beauty" and a thing of "joy," a chronology which is at the same time a poem.

Again, apply to this chronology four or five simple numerals, which, on grounds entirely apart from the chronology, we have ascertained to be used *sometimes* in a mystical way. At once these numerals become a new element of life. They establish a vital connection between the dates of Scripture and its highest poetic flights. The Flood lifts us up to the New Jerusalem. Abraham becomes our teacher in the mystery of the Trinity. Ishmael, after a slumber of two millenniums, wakes and lives again in the Hegira of Mohammed. Nay, the old world before the Flood seems to rise from the dead. Mahalaleel comes before us as the Moses of his age. Enoch testifies against apostasy and schism.

Yet once more, observe how carelessly in appearance, but how systematically when we look at it closely, the chronological chain is broken just at those points where any human contriver of such a scheme would have been least likely to fall into an inadvertence. In the dates of Abraham, Joshua, and Samuel, three most critical epochs, and three names inferior to none other in importance, the connection, so far as the Old Testament goes, is hopelessly impaired. Everything else is given with precision. More than one hundred dates, carefully connected, run through all the books from Genesis to Nehemiah, and show conclusively that the author or authors of those books, whether human or divine, considered chronological accuracy a matter of no little importance. Yet in three most prominent places a flaw occurs in the chain, sufficient to vitiate the whole as a connected chronology. Now, were the Bible a work of human ingenuity, would a blemish so manifest, and so likely to impair its credit in one particular at least, have been allowed to remain? Or if it remained, would it have been in the power of one or two men, living hundreds of years later than its earlier books, to remove the blemish in a way which converts the whole scheme into a perfect harmony? And so with regard to the difficulty in synchronizing the two lines of Ephraim and Judah. There, as we have shown, everything depends upon a mere passing allusion to the fact that Jehoram began to reign, his father *Jehoshaphat being still alive.* So, in another place, a difficulty is removed by the "casual" phrase, in reference to Coniah, that he was carried to Babylon "when the year was expired." And so in numberless other cases, the "inadvertencies" of Scripture have not only the marks of design, but of a design (if one may so speak) to *entrap* the inadvertent reader. And doubtless there are many who allow themselves to be taken in the trap. Not professed skeptics only, but real lovers of the Bible, are often beguiled into the confession that "it is hopeless to make anything of the Bible chronology." I have heard the confession from the lips of genuine scholars, from critics of a high order. When we find, however, that these *seeming* slips of Scripture are carefully provided for, yet in a way that *seems* as casual and inadvertent as the slips themselves; when we learn that the lock is not really deranged, nor the keys mislaid, but that everything is right and in its place, if we only look for it in the right way: then the argument for a divine plan in the *latency* of the Scripture scheme becomes almost irresistible.

The force of this argument will be more clearly seen, if the reader will look back at the symmetries disclosed by the Chronological Table, and see how many of the most wonderful of them are connected with the precise dates of the fall of Jerusalem and of the Dispersion. The 12 "forties"; the 36 "sixty-fives," or the 6 "three hundred and nineties"; the 6 Abrahamic days, the 5 Israel-Judah days, the 4 Jerusalem days; the remarkable "40 times 65," as the measure of the Arphaxad period; the beautiful *average* measure of a "day of preparation"; the equal length of the Antediluvian and Levitical Economies; the 120 of "suspended judgment," and the 600 of "comfort," so exactly repeated; none of these would come out as they do, if the final dates were a little earlier or a little later than they happen to be.

And so again: how was it that St. Stephen, at his martyrdom, a time when one would hardly be expected to care for nice questions of chronology, happened to give us precisely *one* link in the great chain that otherwise might have remained forever a missing link? And how came it that St. Paul, in the most casual way in the world as it would *seem*, *happened* to give the Jews at Antioch in Pisidia another missing link; and that St. Luke, many years afterward, *happened* to report that part of his speech in which he gave it, neglecting (it is probable) many other parts of seemingly more importance? And again, there being another most important link wanting, how did St. Paul chance to give it, by an *obiter dictum*, in a writing so full of other and weighty matters as the Epistle to the Galatians?

The only answer to such questions is that given us by the wise man:* "It is the glory of God to *conceal* a thing." Both in nature and in grace, it hath pleased Him to reveal Himself, indeed, but in such a way as to require, on our parts, a diligent and careful seeking. For, while "it is the glory of God to conceal a thing," it is at the same time "the honor of kings to search out a matter." He hides, that we may seek. The man of

* Prov. xxv, 2.

science, the "king" in the realm of thought, ought to be the last man in the world to dispute this proposition.

4. With this *latent* character of the chronology we may connect the additional and very striking fact, that not merely its symmetry, but in truth its very existence as a chronology, depends on a rigid adherence to the *tenet* of a *plenary* inspiration.

And by this tenet I understand, not perfect accuracy in the Scriptures from *every* point of view, but perfect and entire accuracy from the spiritual point of view.* In other words, when I see a seeming mistake in Scripture, a seeming inadvertency, a seeming contradiction, or the like, faith in plenary inspiration would lead me to doubt my own interpretation rather than the Scripture. It would lead me to look deeper; to scrutinize more closely: and, in the mean time, to regard the difficulty in question, whether I can solve it or not, as part of *the Divine plan* in the grand scheme of inspiration. If one place, for example, seems to contradict another, it is because God *intended* the seeming contradiction. And if a skeptic asks me why He should so intend it, I answer that it may be for the purpose of curing us of shallow self-conceit.

Taking the word, then, in this practical sense, it is remarkable that no sacred chronology can be constructed, *except* on the hypothesis of a plenary inspiration.

---

* I may here be permitted to refer to my *Answer to Bishop Colenso:* in which I started with calling attention to "the spiritual point of view," but had little occasion to adhere to it, inasmuch as that shallow skeptic could be answered very easily on lower grounds. But there are deeper skeptics than Colenso. For their sakes, the fact that the Bible is a book, but *not like other books*, needs to be carefully studied.

The moment we admit, for example, that St. Paul *may* have spoken " inadvertently " in his reference to the " four hundred and thirty years " in the Epistle to the Galatians, we reduce the carefully recorded dates of Scripture to a mere chaos, and no human skill can reconstruct them on a reliable basis.

And, in fact, of the hundreds of chronologies that have been framed from Scripture dates, there is hardly one that does not substitute, in one place or another, a mere conjecture of some sort for a plain Scripture text. Thus one eminent historian rejects St. Paul, because he *seems* to contradict the First book of Kings. But is not an *obiter dictum* of St. Paul as good authority, to say the least, as a mere opinion of a modern interpreter can be? Such devices can never lead to anything reliable. An iron link in a chain of iron cannot be replaced by a link of clay. If there is any such thing as sacred chronology, it must be a chronology in which *every* link is sure, and in which no text of Scripture bearing on the subject is set aside without good reasons.

It may be too much to say that these conditions have been met to a nicety in the Table which has been followed in this Inquiry. Browne, proceeding on the principle here announced, made one mistake: he substituted, in one place, a conjecture for a date. But by that one mistake he vitiated extensively the symmetry of the Table. In the same way the Table here used may prove on a close scrutiny to have fallen short of a perfect adherence to the principle of a plenary inspiration. If so, the analogy would lead me to expect that, *so far as it has fallen short*, it will be found to have vitiated some portion of the fair scheme which in part it has brought out.

In other words, the symmetry of the results obtained by this Inquiry has been *in proportion to the fidelity* with which we have adhered to the tenet of *plenary* inspiration. But a false hypothesis never leads to harmonious results. So far, then, as the results of this Inquiry are beautiful, symmetrical, and harmonious, so far the hypothesis on which it has gone is proved to be a true one.

The argument might be strengthened by going somewhat more into detail. But I have confidence enough in its truth to be willing to leave it, even in this mere outline, to the judgment of the reader.

I must add, however, in justice to the subject, that the narrow limits of this Inquiry necessarily diminish the force and weight of the argument. For the numerals of chronology are but a small section of the numerals of the Bible. And these again are comparatively an insignificant part of a vast system of typology, which, if it were drawn out in its symmetry and completeness, and in a scientific way, would make the study of the Scriptures, what it once was, the most delightful and refreshing as it is the most useful of all studies. Most persons are aware that the Bible abounds in types. But, unfortunately, these types are regarded as matters of mere "fancy." Their endless variety, their harmony and consistency, their entire conformity to ascertainable laws, is hardly even suspected. Hence, modern interpreters either pass them over altogether, or (what is even worse) they admit *a few* of them, with a grave caution to the reader that he must not presume to admit any more than have passed muster with the "judicious commentator," lest perchance he should become "fanciful," like St. Augustine or St. Athanasius.

It seems to me that this subject ought to be taken in hand somewhat more seriously and consistently. *If there are types* in the Old Testament, are these types occasional and accidental only, or are they rather the salient points of some great system which *pervades* the sacred volume? If they are the former, then of course they are unworthy of regard. If the latter be true; if the typical character of Isaac, for example, is elicited by a *principle* of interpretation which, being honestly applied, would be found equally fruitful in the case of Samson, or Daniel, or Jonah, or Enoch, or Elijah, or any other of the great names of sacred history: then we ought to know it, not merely for our own satisfaction, but as a matter of simple justice to that system of interpretation which prevailed for so many ages in the early Church, and by which the theology of the Creed was developed and confirmed, and triumphantly vindicated.

In the mean time, an inquiry into one branch of this subject, unsupported by the results of inquiry in other branches, must labor under the disadvantage of a seeming "novelty," or "fancifulness," or even of presumption.

CHAPTER XVII.

RELATION OF SACRED TO COMMON CHRONOLOGY.

ONE question remains. The Scripture chronology being based, as we have seen, upon symmetrical combinations of certain sacred numbers, what light does this throw upon the system as a matter-of-fact record of the age of man upon the earth?

Browne, in his *Ordo Sæclorum*, sees in the fact a proof that the Mosaic chronology is the only true record of "the times and seasons;" and consequently that the world, at the coming of the Messiah, was only a little more than four thousand years old.

I agree with him in the first proposition. The sacred chronology is a supernatural scheme; it is a divinely inspired record; it has a sanction which no other can reasonably pretend to.

But is it necessarily a record of the lapse or duration of *the whole* of time, of time in the popular and matter-of-fact sense? May it not be a record simply of the *sacred* times, of those "times and seasons" in which God has manifested Himself in a special and extraordinary way?

On a question of such importance I would not dogmatize, nor even go so far as to commit myself to an opinion. The utmost that I would venture would be to indicate briefly a *possible* solution: and this I do, not from any repugnance to what is called "the short chronology," but merely to suggest that in matters of this kind there is room for difference of opinion; that one may have an entire faith in Moses and the Prophets, without feeling in himself any bias whatsoever either for or against the "discoveries" of science.

It seems to me that there is *some ground* for the belief that the sacred chronology is *not* a record of time in general, but only of what may be distinguished as the "*sacred* times."

1. And *first* there is the unquestionable fact that the *genealogies* on which this record is framed may, in accordance with Scripture use, be very much "condensed," without any change in the language which *seems* to mark them as continuous genealogies. Thus St. Matthew says, as plainly as Moses does, that "Abraham *begat* Isaac," and so on down to "Jacob" who "*begat* Joseph, the husband of Mary." Yet he does not hesitate so to frame his series, *by omissions of certain names*, as to make a mystical "*fourteen* generations" for each of the great terms into which his Table is divided. May not Moses have used the same liberty, in Gen. v and xi, with a view to the symmetrical and perhaps mystical scheme of *Ten* which appears in each of those tables?* Such a question cannot be answered by declaiming about the "common sense" and "matter-of-fact" of Englishmen, or Americans, or of the nineteenth century generally. Moses was not an Englishman. That old Shemitic soul which was made the vehicle of inspiration, was not begotten or conceived in "the nineteenth century." We have no right to judge

---

* From Adam to Noah, and from Shem to Abraham.

the Bible by our modern standards, and to say that this or that thing should have been so and so, because *our* arithmetics would have it so and so. God's ways are not as our ways, nor His thoughts as our thoughts. In everything, therefore, that relates to God, whether in His word or in His works, our business is simply to inquire for the facts: to find out *what is*, not what in our impatience we think *ought to be*.

But I am not advocating the theory of "condensed genealogies." I am merely suggesting it. If the reader wishes to inquire into it further, he will find the argument ably and calmly stated in that sound and scholarly work of Professor Green of Princeton, "The Pentateuch vindicated from the aspersions of Colenso."

2. But further: no careful reader of the Bible can fail to have been struck, and perhaps puzzled, by *the geography* and *ethnography* of that sacred Book.

Its *Geography* embraces a small section of the earth's surface, a section of immense importance as being the cradle of religion and civilization, but as compared with the actual habitat of man extremely scant. And even in the New Testament this "earth" is not much enlarged. The Jews who, on the day of Pentecost,* had come together "out of *every nation under heaven*," had indeed assembled from Libya toward the south, from Parthia toward the east, from the south shore of the Black Sea toward the north, and from Rome toward the west. But how large a portion of the earth's surface does that horizon cover? It leaves out of view the bulk of Asia, almost the whole of Africa, the larger portion of Europe, the whole of

---

* Acts ii, 5-11.

America and Australia, to say nothing of the islands scattered over the sea.

Again, the *Ethnography* of the Bible, as given in Genesis x, accounts for the origin of the nations which spread over that small part of the earth's surface just now described; but if we attempt to stretch it so as to cover all tribes on the globe, we are reduced to mere conjecture. Our American Indians, for example, may have come from Shem, or may have come from Ham; and we may even venture to *infer* from the Bible their origin from one of these two sources.* But does the Bible really tell us so? Does it not rather ignore the whole subject? Have we any authority for believing that Noah had *only* three sons? And if we do believe this, have we any ground for our faith, beyond the negative ground of the *silence* of the Scriptures?

Now it seems to me that we are too apt to build upon the silence of Scripture, as if it were actual and positive revelation. Where God does not speak, *we* put in a word; and the word thus put in by ourselves is too apt to be cherished by us as "the sure word" of God.

But the more one studies the Bible, the less inclined he feels to be over positive about things. It is a very deep book. And though there are plenty of people who imagine that they can touch bottom in it, yet it may be in such cases that they are really like children sporting on the sands. It is easy to sound the sea where the sea and shore meet. But if we launch farther out; if we venture forth as it were into the

---

* Gen. ix, 19, would seem to warrant this inference; but the use of the word "*whole* earth" in Scripture is not such as to warrant always a literal interpretation.

silence of the deep; if we reach that point where the horizon bends around us in a circle of infinity, where a whole heaven above smiles upon a whole heaven beneath: then we feel it is high time to put up our fathoming lines, and, confessing our ignorance, to be content with adoration.

And from this point of view I confess I see nothing conclusive in the sacred "times and seasons," so far as the measure of *secular* time goes. As in geography and ethnography there is a *terra incognita* vastly greater in mere bulk than "the earth" which is described, so it may be in the chronology of the Scriptures. There may be tracts of time ignored, ages not syllabled in heaven, patches of darkness and of slumber in the annals of mankind, days when, in the words of an almost inspired Greek,*

> "Seeing, men saw in vain,
> And hearing, heard not, but like dreamy shapes
> Wandered at random all the lingering day,
> An aimless life, nor built them fixed abodes
> Of brick or stone beneath the eye of heaven,
> But burrowing swarmed like ants in sunless caves."

Such times, if such there be, have no record in God's book. They are blotted from His sight. Neither the geography of Scripture nor its ethnography; nor (I venture to think) its chronology, has anything to do with man as a mere animal. When nations become *historic;* when, according to the sublime image of the Prophet,† they come "up out of the sea," and at first as "great beasts," but afterward humanized, being

---

* Æschylus, *Prometh. Vinct.* 447.
† Dan. vii.

made to "stand on their feet as a man" with "a man's heart given" to them, they begin to march in ranks in the ever onward of human progress: then at length they have a part in the Divine Book of Remembrance; then, and not till then, the secular times are made to synchronize with the *sacred* "times and seasons." Before that moment comes, the world in the eye of Scripture is but "the earth" and "the sea." The "earth" alone is sacred. The "sea" is the mixed mass of peoples living confusedly,* without a history and without a name. Yet even in that "sea" a divine power is working. The "living creatures" that it brings forth "abundantly" are destined to emerge. The winged "lion" of Assyria, the "bear" of Persian conquest, the "leopard" of Greek culture, the great and terrible "beast" of Roman arms and laws, each comes out in its turn, each is brought into contact with the light of the true religion, each begins to have its record in sacred chronology.

"But all this is mere theory." Of course, it is nothing more. No one is bound to believe it. No one is bound to respect it. Still, it may serve to illustrate the fact, that the history of the human race is a large and deep subject; and that, in reference to its chronology as to many other matters, there is room for much inquiry and for honest differences of opinion.

3. There are some positive intimations, slight indeed but very significant, that the Scripture Record of "the times and seasons" may be, not, as it seems at first, a measure of all time, but rather a series of stepping stones over a vast sea of silence.

* The extent to which this typical meaning of "earth" and "sea" may be traced in Scripture is both striking and edifying.

The term in Paradise, the term of Joshua's "rest," and some others of like character happen to be *undated*. To a full believer in Inspiration this cannot be considered a matter of mere chance. It is a phenomenon of that kind which almost forces one to think. And if one begins to pause and think, the first thought which arises is that the omission in these places is not according to the wont of ordinary chronology. For common history has always a fellow feeling for human curiosity. What we particularly want to know, it particularly tries to tell us. Yet the Bible, telling us a thousand things which comparatively have little interest to us, leaves a gap precisely in those places where a word of information would be like a drop of water to a fevered tongue. How long did Adam live in Paradise? Who would not rather know that, than to learn how old Enoch was when he begat Methuselah?

These gaps in the chronology, then, have certainly a mystic look about them. And though they are covered, so far as the general scheme goes, by subsequent utterances of Scripture, yet the very *covering* has something of the same mystic look. The Book of Kings implies "Seven" for "Joshua's rest;" St. Paul seems to allow "Sixty." Which is the matter of fact number? Or is either a number of mere matter of fact? *

It may be said, however, that Daniel's "seventy weeks of years" proved arithmetically exact; and finding a literal exactness in that case, and a continuous succession of the "weeks," we are bound to believe in a similar exactness and a like continuity in all the other "times and seasons."

* See p. 32.

It may be so. Yet, among all the commentators who have explored that term of history, and who have so ably demonstrated the fulfilment of the prophecy, I find not one who can fix precisely *the last half week* of the Prophet's seventy. The other terms come out, as I have shown, with miraculous precision. But when we look for some marked and dated event to close the last and critical term, we are suddenly left in a kind of haze. Hence the ablest commentators regard this "half week" as a term reserved, a term by itself, a term germinating as it were for the Day of Antichrist. I have little doubt that this theory is the true one. But, so far as it is true, it shows a mystic element in the Scriptural terms of years. They are not like common years. Or if in some respects they are like common years, if to a certain extent they are found to synchronize with profane chronology, yet there is something over and above this; there are certain features in which the sacred record differs decidedly from all others.

But, besides this, even if sacred chronology in its later terms is found to agree with the dates of ordinary history, it does not follow that the same must be true of its prehistoric terms. Whatever may be the age of the world, or the length of time it has been inhabited by man, there can be no doubt that *history*, in any true sense of the word, is quite a modern thing. Even the Egyptians have no early history worthy of the name. There is, therefore, a broad line of demarcation between the earlier ages of the world and the later ages. In the later, history has developed. In the earlier, everything is buried beneath mountains of oblivion. The Bible alone gives us some record of those ages.

But whether this record is meant to be continuous, or is merely a summary of such periods as are particularly worth recording, we are not expressly informed; and so far as there are intimations on the subject, even these are of a character that may be variously interpreted.

4. The alteration of the chronology by the Septuagint translators is a very curious fact, and seems to me to have a bearing in connection with this subject.

That the figures in the earlier parts of the Bible were by them deliberately and systematically altered, so as to lengthen the historic period by nearly fifteen hundred years, is now admitted, I believe, by all competent inquirers.* But how could they venture on so daring an enterprise? How, as learned and devout Jews, could they reconcile it to their conscience? How could the mass of their co-religionists acquiesce in it? How could the alteration receive at least the tacit sanction both of the Jews and early Christians?

I can account for it only in one way. The chronology of the Patriarchal period could not have been regarded as a literal measure of all time; it must have been looked upon as a mystical or sacred measure. In other words, the Jews, or at least a large body of their interpreters, must have regarded the *meaning* of the Scripture numbers in the light of an open question. If they took that view of the subject, we can readily understand how, in interpreting to the Greeks, they should have taken the liberty of translating in accordance with Greek ideas. But on any other supposition their course is inexplicable; and the conduct of their countrymen in acquiescing in their work, is more inexplicable still.

* Browne demonstrates it beyond all reasonable question.

Of course this does not prove that the Seventy were right in thus altering the Numerals. It seems to indicate, however, that they had a certain warrant for it in the traditions of their school; and that, however jealous they might be of the slightest alteration in the sacred Original, they did not feel themselves bound by the letter of that Original, but were free to interpret it by the best light they could get. *To reduce the sacred times to the measure of ordinary times*, must have needed, in their opinion, a free handling of the figures.

Such facts are not of sufficient weight to settle the question we are considering. Still, they are not altogether destitute of force. They may serve at least to keep us from an over-hasty judgment.

But, it may be urged, does not uncertainty on this point necessarily lead one to doubt the character of the Scriptures in general? Especially if the numerals of Scripture Chronology are so peculiarly symmetrical, if they are framed upon *a system* of spiritual instruction such as has been described, will not this fact be an argument against the *historical* character of the events connected with this chronology?

I answer, that if the system were *natural*, so that it could be accounted for on any theory of human ingenuity, the argument undoubtedly would have much weight. But if we have proved anything, we have proved it to be supernatural. It is a system devised by One, who can bring about events as easily as He can inspire dates. The fact, then, that historical events do not fall naturally into any symmetrical arrangement of "times and seasons," weighs nothing against the historical character of the events connected with the Biblical Chronology; it merely shows that Bible History is not like ordinary history, but, in one important point, differs from it materially. For ordinary history relates natural events occurring in the order of nature; Bible history dwells mainly on supernatural events occurring in the order of Grace. That there should be a symmetry and significance in the latter, which we do not discover in the former, is precisely what on *à priori* grounds we might reasonably expect.

But over and above this, we are by no means sure that the order and sequence of ordinary history would not be found as symmetrical as those of sacred history,* if only we were in a position to contemplate the subject as a whole.

* I have tried many of the prominent dates of ordinary Christian History, for example, the great Persecutions, the principal Emperors, Councils, Popes, by the same tests which have been applied to the Sacred Chronology. The results are very curious. *First*, out of some 30 *epochs* of what I may distinguish as *Japhetic* history, I find *not one* that divides by any of the sacred factors with any appreciable significance. *Secondly*, out of 17 prominent dates, connected with Jewish and Saracen history, and which I may distinguish as *Shemitic*, all are divisible by sacred factors with entire appropriateness. Some of these are 4194, the end of Jerusalem, divisible by 6; 4224, the end of S. John, the last of the *Judaic* foundation stones, divisible by 6 and by 8 times 8; 4256, the year of Bar Cochbas, see Chap. xv; 4693 (A. D. 569), the birth of Mohammed, divisible by 13; 4746, the Hegira, divisible by 42; or if we take the interval between that date and 2107, the year of Ishmael's circumcision, divisible by 13; 4758 (A. D. 634), the year of Caliph Omar, the first inroads into Syria; 4771 (A. D. 647), the Saracen conquests in Africa; 4784 (660), beginning of great Mohammedan schism; 4836 (712), fall of the Gothic monarchy in Spain before the Saracens; 5577 (1453), fall of Constantinople; 5616 (1492), the expulsion of the Moors from Spain: all these, divisible by 13. From the analogy suggested by these instances, I was led to suspect that *two* dates of the church, *intimately con-*

Science has advanced but a few steps in the great work of arranging and classifying the phenomena of common life. But so far as it has advanced, all inquiry goes to prove that everything happens according to fixed laws, nothing according to chance. Given a certain number of human beings, living in a certain way, and the number of births, marriages, or deaths among them, nay even the number of crimes of any particular description, can be calculated with great precision. Had we a larger number of *data*, more accurately classified, the calculation might be made with greater precision still. It thus appears that even human liberty is under a law. Man's goings are ordered. The very hairs of his head are numbered. *L'homme propose, Dieu dispose.* There is a Divinity that shapes our ends, rough hew them as we may. The only real progress of science is that which goes to establish these maxims of common sense, and to prove laboriously what has long since been divined by the human heart.

But what common sense has divined, and science goes to prove, has been authoritatively announced and beautifully illustrated by Divine revelation. "God created Wisdom, and saw her, and *numbered* her, and poured her upon all His works." There is no such thing as chance in God's world—no such thing as con-

nected *with Jerusalem and Judaism,* would also divide by 13. Julian's *apostasy* was marked by an effort to restore the Temple: the first great Arian Council, that condemned S. Athanasius and practically rejected the Nicene creed, was held *in Jerusalem,* at the dedication of the Church of the Holy Sepulchre. Accordingly I tried these dates, and found that the year of Julian, 4485 (361), and the year of the Council of Tyre and Jerusalem, 4459 (335), both divide by 13, with very significant quotients. Compare these results with those in Appendix B.

fusion. Everything is numbered, everything is in its place, everything comes up in its time and season. As the wise man says, "He hath made everything beautiful in his time." Upon nature and upon history there is the stamp of symmetry and proportion. But "He hath set the world in their hearts, so that no man can find out the work that God maketh from the beginning to the end." We are bewildered by the multiplicity of things. In history especially, there seems at first sight nothing but a grand phantasmagoria of facts and dates. But were we at as great a distance from human actions as we are from the stars, doubtless we should see as much of order in the one as in the other. Indeed, to the common eye, the stars themselves are scattered loosely over the expanse of heaven. It is science that brings order out of the seeming confusion. It is science which enables us to see what the Bible told us thousands of years ago, that God "telleth the number of the stars, and calleth them all by their names."

And by a like anticipation of the results of scientific inquiry, the Bible informs us that our steps are numbered; that our days are numbered; that the hairs of our head are all numbered; nay, that God numbereth the drops of rain; that the righteous are numbered to life, that the wicked are numbered to the sword; that earthly kingdoms are numbered: and, in short, that there is nothing without number, save only "His understanding," of which the Psalmist declares "there is no number."

There is a peculiar propriety, therefore, in the question which I have placed on the title page of this book:* "Why else is He styled PALMONI by the

* See the rich and racy introduction to the "Book of Num-

Prophet Daniel? . . . Which is rendered, I confess, in our running translations by '*that certain saint*'; but in the margin of our English Bibles by the *Numberer of Secrets*, or the *Wonderful Numberer:* as if Palmoni were a compound . . . in which is retained the name of *Wonderful*, a name of Christ, . . . as well as of *Counsellor*."

God, indeed, is a "Wonderful Numberer." So far, then, as it has been shown by this Inquiry that the sacred chronology is full of symmetry, beauty, and significance, even in its numerals, so far we have proved, not that the Bible is in any way unhistorical, but that it is history of a vastly higher kind than anything else that we are accustomed to call by that name. It is the ideal of history. It is what even common history might be, if it were written from a higher point of view, and with a more perfect knowledge of "the work that God maketh."

When the history of the Christian era comes to be written, not by shallow rationalists who are afraid to lift up their eyes to heaven, lest they should be mistaken for believers, but by men of real science and real faith, its periods and dates and sequences of events may fall into an order as striking, as beautiful, as harmonious, as that which seems to pervade the Hebrew chronology.

In the mean time we can rest upon one conclusion. Whether the sacred chronology be a record of common time or not, it is at all events a record of God's times.

bers" in the 4th vol. of the *Bibliotheca Biblica*. I may observe, in reference to the word *Palmoni*, that its numerical value is 80, 30, 40, 6, 50, 10, or 216, which is the *Three* times *Three* times *Three* multiplied by *Eight:* a most significant combination.

It bears upon it the marks of the supernatural. Nay, it not only proves itself, but it also goes far to prove the Inspiration and Divine Authority of the Scriptures in general.

Knowing this to be the case, we are able to learn much from it, though on some points there may be more or less of uncertainty. Especially we may learn much, and be not a little comforted, with regard to spiritual things. As to secular and earthly matters, the gratification of curiosity or the acquisition of mere knowledge, we are not so sure that the Bible was intended for our instruction. The time of man upon the earth, like the age of the earth itself, is a question of human science. To science we may leave the solution of the problem. And, in the mean time, while the question is still in doubt, while investigations are going on that may confirm or may dispel the theories now current on the subject, it is not wise to commit the Bible to more than it positively and undoubtedly affirms. Where it speaks, we bow to it implicitly. Where it is silent, we bow also, but in humble expectancy, waiting for more light.

APPENDIX A.

BISHOP BUTLER AND ISAAC WILLIAMS.

Bishop Butler, in his Analogy, Part II. Ch. VII, makes the following remarks upon that kind of *circumstantial* evidence, depending for its weight upon a large accumulation of analogies or correspondences, which makes *Prophecy* one great branch of the proof of Inspiration in the Scriptures:

"It plainly requires a degree of modesty and fairness, beyond what every one has, for a man to say, not to the world, but to himself, *that there is a real appearance of somewhat of great weight in this matter,* though he is not able thoroughly to satisfy himself about it; *but it shall have its influence upon him, in proportion to its appearing reality and weight.* It is much more easy, and more falls in with the negligence, presumption and wilfulness of the generality, *to determine at once,* with a decisive air, *that there is nothing in it.*

"But the truth of our religion, like the truth of common matters, is to be judged of by *all the evidence taken together.* And unless the whole series of things which may be alleged in this argument, and every particular thing in it, *can reasonably be supposed to have been by accident, (for here the stress of the argument for Christianity lies,)* then is the truth of it proved.

"It is obvious how much advantage the nature of this evidence gives to those persons who attack Christianity, especially in conversation. For it is easy to show, in a short and lively manner, that *such and such things are liable to objection,* that *this and another thing is of little weight in itself;* but impossible to show, in like manner, the united force of the whole argument in one view."

The argument in this Inquiry is in some parts so strictly mathematical that it stands in little need of the wise Bishop's apology. It needs it thus far, however, that its force depends upon an accumulation of facts all pointing in the same direction; but to give all the facts, or anything like all, would exhaust the patience of any but the most studious readers.

As I have said in the Preface, I do not wish to put anything advanced in this book *on the ground of authority;* and I have, therefore, abstained from any reference to the early Church writers. To show, however, that I have advanced no "novelties," at least so far as the general *principle* is concerned, I make the following extract from one who admirably reflects the Patristic mind, the Rev. Isaac Williams. In his *Thoughts on the Study of the Holy Gospels*, he observes, Part IV, Section I:

"The cases of analogy which occur in (Holy Scripture) are so numerous, so manifold, and so remarkable, that *it seems to intimate something of a vast system*, of which these are but the casual intimations; consequently that *greater light in things Divine will consist in a fuller observation of these analogies.*

"For instance, *the course of time* in which we are placed is entirely regulated by the law of analogy; every portion of it is but the return of similar periods ...... And on this analogy in the periods of time depend an infinite variety of other analogies, by which the natures of all living creatures are regulated, the renewal, the decay, and changes of all creation; *for all these are governed by, and depend upon, seasons of time.* And, moreover, this analogy of time in things natural is connected also with what is spiritual and Divine by Holy Scripture. As for instance, in the appointment of the Sabbath:—the seventh day, the seventh year, the seven times seventh. Nor is it possible to say, *to what extent this may reach, or how far it may regulate the Divine proceedings;* as was the case in the duration of the Captivity being regulated by Sabbatical periods of time, *till the land had enjoyed her Sabbaths.*

"Another order of analogy may be observed in things natural, in objects greatly differing in size and importance ...... The periods of a state or nation form a resemblance to the four ages of human life, its infancy, gradual rise, completion, and decay. So also in the living creatures that come to our notice, small objects will appear to be formed after the model of larger ones, and in some degree to represent them in miniature; or *parts of the same object will be similar in formation to the whole,* as a branch of the tree to the entire tree. So that if in Holy Scripture the history of a nation and an individual, or the Church and a Christian, are types of each other, it would appear to be according to the same law of analogy: or that *the courses of events,* as they proceed, *should be developing similar circles, similar appearances, forms,* or *shadows of form,* in matters infinitely differing in importance.

"These three numbers, seven, and forty, and twelve, may serve *as some slight indication of a hidden analogy of numbers,* by which successive periods of time may be regulated." *Thoughts,* &c., pp. 199–208.

What this thoughtful writer intimates as possible, with regard to *three* numbers, the preceding Inquiry shows to be in the highest degree probable with regard to them and to several others like them. The process by which the fact is brought out may be objected to; but that the "successive periods" of the Hebrew Chronology are "regulated" by such numbers as seven, eight, five, nine, twelve, forty, thirteen, sixty-five, and the like, stands before us as a simple and well-warranted fact.

I may here observe, in passing, that the relations of Scripture numerals might be largely *illustrated*—at least, so I think from a cursory examination of the subject—by a close study of the analogous relations of numbers in sound, light, and chemical combinations. To do justice to this subject, however, would require more knowledge of Optics, Acoustics, and the like, than I can pretend to.

To the well weighed words of Butler and Williams, I add a brief extract from "The Types of Genesis, by Andrew Jukes," a Scotch Presbyterian clergyman: a work of some merit in this line, but rather sentimental, and sadly deficient in precision of ideas:

"As to the form of the Old Testament, Jerome notices that the number of the books, according to the Jewish division (*five* books of the Law, *eight* of the Prophets, and *nine* of the Hagiographa), answers exactly to the *twenty-two* letters of the Hebrew alphabet; and that, as there are five double letters in the Hebrew, so there are five double books, namely, two Samuels, two Kings, two Chronicles, two Ezras (which we call Ezra and Nehemiah), and two Jeremiahs (that is, Jeremiah and the Lamentations). The fact that part of the book of Proverbs (chap. xxxi, 10–31), the whole of the Lamentations, and seven Psalms (namely, the xxv, xxxiv, xxxvii, cxi, cxii, cxix, and cxlv), are *acrostics*, founded on the Hebrew alphabet, leads him to suppose that there is some mystery in these twenty-two sounds, which form all words, connected with the comprehensive character of the word. Modern criticism may smile, but there is far more in this than appears at first sight."

A large amount of Patristic testimony might be added: but believing the subject to be one which the modern mind must study out for itself, and in its own way, and which the modern mind (if it should really become interested in it) might do much to illustrate, I content myself with the above indications of what studious men have thought and said. As to what men have said who have never taken the trouble to think on the subject,—and I fear many modern "commentators" are in that category,—it is hardly worth while to inquire.

APPENDIX B.

MINOR DETAILS OF SACRED CHRONOLOGY.

The remarkable uniformity with which the numbers Seven, Eight, Nine and Thirteen, divide into such dates only as are easily associated with the type ideas of those numerals, indicates a law which one would hardly expect to hold good for more than the salient points of the sacred Chronology. A larger experiment, however, shows that the coincidence has a wider application. From the birth of Seth to the decree of Artaxerxes there are more than 100 dates or terms in the regular series. I have tried all these with the following results:

The number *Thirteen*, dividing first into the date of Seth, "when men began to call upon the Name of the Lord," the era of the first *separation* between the "sons of God" and the "children of men," continues to be the prominent factor of various dates at intervals to the time of Noah: then, *Eight* becomes prominent, and divides successively into *every* date and term, without exception: into 1056, Noah's birth; 480, the interval between that event and the "suspended judgment;" 1536, the epoch of suspended judgment; 120, the term of suspended judgment, "while the ark was a-preparing;" and 1656, the year of the Flood.

Now, the *Apostasy* of the world before the Flood began with Cain. But there are no dates in Cain's line. The Thirteen must appear, therefore, if at all, in the chronology of the sacred line. And there accordingly it does appear. But it appears, precisely as the *principle* of sacred numbers would require—supposing that *there is* a principle,—in combination with the *Ten* of the commandments or the *Five* of the Law. Thus, Seth's date is 13 times 10: and after living 105 years, which is 65 and 40, he begets Enos: and "*then* men began to call on the Name of the Lord." And so it continues, with various combinations of the same number, to the "days of Noah." *Then* it suddenly stops, and *Eight* takes its place. Afterward, it reappears, and always in a significant way, so as to emphasize from time to time the successive outbreaks of the spirit of apostasy, self-will, or schism. Thus, I find it in connection with Joktan's era; with that of Abimelech (the usurper in the days of the Judges); with the death of Saul; with the reign of Uzziah, who in his latter days intruded into the priests' office, and "was smitten with leprosy;" with the apostasy of Joash.

To bring this out more distinctly, I will give the details of the Chronology of the World before the Flood: see Gen. v.

A. M.		PROMINENT EVENTS.
130	or 13 × 10,	Seth born, in place of Abel, whom Cain slew.
105	" 65 + 40,	" lives and begets Enos.
235		Enos born: then began men to call upon the Name of the Lord.
90		
325	" 5 × 5 × 13,	Cainan.
70		
395		Mahalaleel, who lives to the year 1290, or 3 × 430.
65	" 5 × 13.	
460		Jared.
162		
622		Enoch, translated 987, 13 years before the end of the first Millennium.
65	" 5 × 13.	
687		Methuselah.
187		
874		Lamech.
182	" 14 × 13.	
1056	" 11 × 12 × 8,	Noah born.

A. M.	PROMINENT EVENTS.
480 or 60 × 8.	
1536 " 3 × 8 × 8 × 8,	...Era of Suspended Judgment.
120 " 15 × 8.	
1656 " 207 × 8,	.........The Flood.

Here the Thirteen, beginning in connection with Ten, the number of the commandments or the number of infinity, ends in connection with twice the Seven of "rest:" then, Eight follows, in the most marked way, as the chief factor of *five* numerals in succession.

The next great period, the middle pair of Days, gives dates and numbers which are full of significance if reckoned from Arphaxad, but, if reckoned from the Creation, of no particular meaning. Thus, Abraham's day is 450, or *nine* Jubilees. Isaac's, the birth of Jacob and Esau, is 510 from Arphaxad or 512 from the Flood: in the one, 15, in the other, 8, being prominent factors. In the birth of Jacob, however, the A. M. date is also divisible by the Eight of resurrection. There are many other curious combinations of sacred numbers in the figures of this line. I give the dates according to both reckonings.

1658	Arphaxad	0 or	0.
1693	Salah	35 "	7 × 5.
1723	Eber	65 "	13 × 5.
1757	Peleg	99 "	3 × 33.
1787	Reu	129 "	3 × 43.
1819	Serug	161 "	7 × 23.
1849	Nahor	191.	
1878	Terah	220 "	11 × 20.
2083	Abram's call	425 "	25 × 17.
2108	Abraham	450 "	9 × 50.
2168 or 8 × 271	Jacob and Esau born	510 "	15 × 2 × 17.
2298	Joseph and Jacob in Egypt	640 "	8 × 80.
2538	Exodus	880 "	8 × 110.

Here, again, the presence of the Thirteen in connection

with Eber, whose son Joktan separated from the sacred family and became an element of the Saracen power, is remarkable: also, the predominance of the Dominical number in the dates of Isaac and Jacob. It may also be noticed that the "few and evil days" of Jacob, before he went down into Egypt, the times of wrestlings and strugglings, and family feuds and divisions, are 130 years, a multiple of Thirteen.

In the next period, we enter upon the Levitical Dispensation, the anti-type of the world before the Flood; and the significant dates seem to fall again into the regular series, reckoned from the Creation. Their precise application in each particular instance is not so obvious as in some cases that we have considered. There can be no doubt, however, that the *twelve* Judges and *six* Servitudes, interrupted for a little more than 3 years by the apostasy and usurpation of Abimelech, make up a period of sacred history eminently typical: the Judges being *saviours* specially raised up by God, and the Theocracy existing in its simplest and purest form. Moreover, Samson, the twelfth of these "saviours," is more richly and manifoldly than any other character of the Old Testament a type of the Saviour as *a warrior, spoiling principalities and powers*. It is also noticeable that the 450 years of Judges (including 60 years of Joshua and the Elders) can be divided into 336 years of "rest," which is 7 times 48; and 114 years of oppression, which is 6 times 19: or, if we leave out the term of Joshua, there are 276 years for the 12 Judges, or 12 times 23. In short, the character of this period being considered, it is not surprising that the Abrahamic number of judgment and deliverance, or (in the broad sense of the word) the "baptismal number" Nine, should be prominent at its beginning and at its close; and that there should also be a marked presence of the Dominical and Sabbatical numerals.

The dates in this period would be difficult to adjust, were it not for the summary of them given by S. Paul. With the help of that summary, we arrange them as follows:

2638.	First Servitude: Cushan Rishathaim.
2646 or $7 \times 7 \times 9 \times 2 \times 3$.	First Judge, Othniel: 40 years of deliverance.
2686.	Second Servitude: Eglon of Moab.
2704 " 8×338.	Second Judge, Ehud, and Third Judge, Shamgar: a period of 80 years.
2784 " $8 \times 4 \times 3 \times 29$.	Third Servitude: Sisera.
2804 " 4×701.	Fourth Judge, Barak.
2844 " $4 \times 9 \times 79$.	Fourth Servitude: Midianites.
2851.	Fifth Judge, Gideon.
2891 " $7 \times 7 \times 59$.	Abimelech, the Usurper—3 years.
2894.	Sixth Judge, Tola.
2917.	Seventh Judge, Jair.
2939.	Fifth Servitude.
2957.	Eighth Judge, Jephthah.
2963.	Ninth Judge, Ibzan.
2970 " $9 \times 3 \times 110$.	Tenth Judge, Elon.
2980.	Eleventh Judge, Abdon.
2988 " $9 \times 4 \times 83$.	Sixth Servitude: Philistines.
3008 " $8 \times 8 \times 47$.	Twelfth Judge, Samson, dies.
3028.	Day of Mizpeh: Samuel and Saul.

In this period, the numbers Seven, Eight, Nine, Twelve, or Four and Three, cannot be distinctly associated with particular names, except in the case of Samson; but they occur in a way appropriate to the general type character of the period, and (possibly) a closer study might reveal a stricter propriety in their recurrence. As it is, it may be worth noticing, in a "free inquiry" and in connection with symmetries already alluded to, that the Fours, the Sevens, the Eights, and the Nines, appear each four times as factors, while the Three appears three times. In an "inquiry," it is well to notice things, whether we attach to them any importance, or not.

In the era of the Kings, there is no date for Saul. He, like Cain, is ignored in Sacred Chronology. His last year, however, is the first of David; and in that, *Thirteen* appears as a prominent factor. In the next date, which is that of David in Jerusalem, the numbers Three and Five, or Five and Fifteen, are conspicuous. Another appearance of *Thirteen* is in connection with Uzziah, whose apostasy was one of a very marked character, and was terribly avenged. It is remarkable that this king reigned 52 years, which is 4 times 13: also, that Jeroboam II, his great contemporary, reigned 40 years in prosperity, followed by 12 years of anarchy and apostasy, which makes again 52 years or 4 times 13. This, moreover, is the beginning of those 65 years of disintegration predicted by the prophet Isaiah.*

Seven comes out in the date of Solomon; of Jotham, who like Solomon was a great builder of "the House of the Lord," 2 Chron. xxvii; and of the year 3563, when the first "rest" or relief occurred in the Captivity. For in that year, being "the *seven* and thirtieth year of the captivity of Jehoiachin king of Judah, in the twelfth month, on the *seven* and twentieth day of the month," the king of Babylon "did lift up the head of Jehoiachin king of Judah out of prison; and he spake kindly to him .... and changed his prison garments: and he did eat bread continually before him all the days of his life:" 2 Kings xxv, 27.

The Resurrection number appears in the reign of Asa, whose time was a great *revival* and *restoration* of the true religion: 2 Chron. xv, 1–15. It comes out also, as before noticed, in the date of the restoration or resurrection of the Temple.

The year of Athaliah, that year of judgment and of a bloody baptism, when Jehu slew all of the house of Ahab, with the princes of Judah, and Athaliah "destroyed all the seed royal of the house of Judah," 2 Chron. xxii, Joash alone being stolen by his sister "*from among the king's sons that were slain,*" and being "hid in the house of God," whence he afterward emerged as one risen from the dead: this marked year in the sacred calendar is 3240, or 9 times 9 times 8 times 5. Moreover it was in his *seventh* year that Joash began to reign: and so long as Jehoiada the priest lived, he walked in the steps

---

* Is. vii, 8

of David and Solomon, and repaired the House of the Lord. But about a year before his death, having reigned 39, or thrice *thirteen* years, Jehoiada died, being 130, or ten times *thirteen* years old; and the king *apostatized*, and he and his princes "left the house of the Lord God of their fathers, and served groves and idols;" and they conspired against Zechariah the son of Jehoiada, who rebuked their wickedness, "and stoned him with stones *at the commandment of the king* in the court of the house of the Lord." And when Zechariah "died, he said, The Lord look upon it, and require it." So Joash also died within a year; his servants having conspired against him and slain him "for the blood of the sons of Jehoiada the priest:" 2 Chron. xxiii, xxiv. This eventful tragedy, with its baptism into death, its rest in the House of God, its joyful resurrection, its restoration of the Law, its repairing of the Temple, its final apostasy and awful catastrophe, seems to draw into itself all the sacred numbers. The *Nine* twice repeated, the *Eight*, the *Five*, the *Seven*, the *Forty*, the *Thirteen* appearing in two ways, seem to wait upon it like a mystic chorus, pointing its moral, or intimating in dumb show the presence of supernatural powers behind the scene.

The chronology of the whole period is as follows:

3068 or 13×236.		End of Saul, and beginning of David's reign.
3075 "	$15 \times 5 \times 41$.	David in Jerusalem.
3108 "	7×444.	Solomon.
3118.		The Temple.
3148.		Jeroboam and Rehoboam.
3165.		Abijam.
3168 "	$8 \times 9 \times 44$.	Asa: a great Revival or Restoration.
3209.		Jehoshaphat.
3239.		Ahaziah.
3240 "	$8 \times 9 \times 9 \times 5$.	Athaliah: the great year of Judgment and Deliverance.
3246.		Joash.
3286.		Amaziah.
3300 "	3×1100.	Jeroboam II, of Israel, recovers the ancient borders.

3315 or 13 × 255.	Uzziah, apostate and smitten with leprosy.
3367 " 7 × 481.	Jotham; a great builder, &c. 2 Chron. xxvii.
3383.	Ahaz.
3399 " 3 × 1133.	Hezekiah.
3428.	Manasseh: sinned, but repented.
3483 " 9 × 9 × 46.	Amon inherits his father's sin, and judgment comes upon him: he is slain in his own house. 2 Chron. xxxiii.
3485.	Josiah: the pious king, who began to reign when 8 years old, and reigned 31 years—the numbers of resurrection and of Deity. But, together, they make 39, or 3 times 13. Moreover, in the 13th year of Josiah, Jeremiah began to prophesy against the apostasy of Judah—giving us the date that follows.
3497 " 13 × 269.	The 13th of Josiah, when Jeremiah began to prophesy.
3516.	Jehoiakim.
3518.	The Captivity.
3527.	Zedekiah.
3538.	Destruction of the Temple.
3563 " 75 × 09.	Rest or Relief in the Captivity: Jehoiachin "lifted up."
3588 " 13 × 276.	Persian power in Babylon: Cyrus's Decree.
3608 " 8 × 451.	Temple restored.
3665 " 5 × 733.	Decree of Artaxerxes.

To these may be added a few dates from common history, at the end of our Table. For example, Herod's reign has *Nine* as a factor. Considering the character of this reign; that it was the execution of the judgment of the sceptre departing from Judah, that from beginning to end it was bathed in blood, that it terminated with the Nativity, the Martyrdom of the Holy Innocents, and the "baptism into death" of "the young child;" the propriety of the number Nine is obvious enough. John Baptist's date, as calculated by Dr. Jarvis, divides by Seven: being thus in the same category with the end of Enoch and Elijah. The presence of sacred numbers in the Antichristian dates is consistent with the Antichrist idea. For Antichrist is a *spiritual* power. It not only opposes, it *counterfeits* Christ. So far as I have examined, however, I find no appropriate use of Sacred numbers, except in the *Shemitic* chronology. When I try European history, a coincidence may come up here or there, but there is no uniformity, no consistency. I may add, that the two Antichrist numerals, *Thirteen* and *Forty-two*, are both made up of Seven and Six. The one is 7 and 6, the earthly added to the heavenly; the other is 7 times 6, the heavenly multiplied into the earthly: in both, there is the mixture or confusion of things sacred and profane.

The following are marked dates of Moslem history: the Hegira, divisible by 42 with one hundred and *thirteen* as a quotient; Mohammed born 569 A. D.; John the Faster of Constantinople, who on account of his assumption of the title *Universal Bishop* was declared to be "the forerunner of Antichrist," consecrated 582, *thirteen* years after the birth of Mohammed, occupied the Episcopal throne *thirteen* years—his accession having taken place, moreover, just 40 years before the Hegira; 634, Caliph Omar the first Moslem Conqueror; 647, Moslem conquest of Africa; 660, death of Ali; 712, Conquest of Spain, Witiza, whose folly and wickedness led to that overthrow, having come to the throne just *thirteen* years before; 1453, Fall of Constantinople; 1492, Expulsion from Spain, after 60 times 13 years of occupation; 1830, Algiers rescued from Moslem rule; 1856, Settlement (for the time being) of the "Eastern Question." All these dates, reduced to years of the World, divide by Thirteen; and in connection with some of them, the fateful number comes out in two or three ways.

APPENDIX C.

I have observed, p. 117, that the number *Six* is a factor of the "two great finial epochs." I find, on closer examination, that this is true, and in a very remarkable way, of *all* the dates which have a decidedly terminal character within the two great finial periods.

Thus, within the 600 years before the Flood, there are precisely *six* dates divisible by Six: 1056, the birth of Noah, which may be considered the end of Adam's Day; 1140, the end of Enos, the third person; 1290, the end of Mahalaleel, the fifth; 1422, the end of Jared, the father of Enoch; 1536, when God said "The end of all flesh is come before me," Gen. vi. 3, 13; and 1656, when the end came in the Flood.

So, within the 600 years before the Flood of the Judaic War and the final desolation, there are precisely six dates divisible by Six, all of a marked terminal character: 3588, the end of the Captivity; 3714, the end of Prophecy and Vision; 4074, the end of insurrection against the Romans, the beginning of Cæsar's power; 4086, the beginning of Herod, and the end of Judah's power—"the sceptre" departing "from Judah;" 4152, the end of our Lord's Ministry; 4194, the end of Temple worship.

In both these periods, the marked *terms* of years are also divisible by Six: in Noah's, the 480, 120, and 600; in the other period, the 120, the 600, and the final 6 years of the Judaic war.

It is also remarkable that the year of the Hegira, which is the *terminus* of that germinating "70 weeks" of Daniel, also has Six as a factor. The same is true of the year 100 (4224), the end of S. John, the last of the Apostles.

THE END.

www.ingramcontent.com/pod-product-compliance
Lightning Source LLC
Chambersburg PA
CBHW032157160426
43197CB00008B/952